THE ***PD's*** | P‍ _____ lls
f‍ _____
of English

Edith Crowell Trager
Sara Cook Henderson

Prentice-Hall, Inc., Englewood Cliffs, New Jersey 07632

Printed in the United States of America

10 9 8 7 6 5 4

ISBN 0-13-730920-1

Editors
Pat Campbell
Dennis Oliver

Prentice-Hall International, Inc., *London*
Prentice-Hall of Australia Pty. Limited, *Sydney*
Editora Prentice-Hall do Brasil, Ltda., *Rio de Janeiro*
Prentice-Hall Canada Inc., *Toronto*
Prentice-Hall of India Private Limited, *New Delhi*
Prentice-Hall of Japan, Inc., *Tokyo*
Prentice-Hall of Southeast Asia Pte. Ltd., *Singapore*
Whitehall Books Limited, *Wellington, New Zealand*

CONTENTS

Authors' Foreword

It is a real effort for us to think back to a time when *The Pronunciation Drills* did not exist. However, making that effort, we remember that we were working at the American Language Center of the American University in Washington, D.C., one of us (Mrs. Trager) as a developer of materials and the other (Mrs. Henderson) as a classroom teacher. Dr. Alva L. Davis was director of the Language Center at that time, and the student body was made up largely of foreign business and professional people who had received grants to study in the United States, plus diplomats, or members of their families, who were stationed in Washington, D.C. As we worked with these students, we heard many stories about misunderstandings caused by mispronunciations, such as that of the young speaker of Spanish who tried repeatedly to order hot milk at breakfast, and was always served oatmeal.

When we looked for materials to use in working with the pronunciation problems of students from various language backgrounds, we found very few which seemed to fill our students' needs. With the encouragement and help of Dr. Davis, we decided to develop our own. We wrote an experimental version that teachers at the American Language Center used for a year or so; then, with their suggestions and criticisms in mind, we refined the text and wrote the final version. It was published in 1956 by English Language Services (now ELS Publications) and, along with the tapes that accompany it, has been a steady seller to both individuals and institutions ever since. This text has become, so they tell us, a classic.

It has been a steady pleasure to meet a stream of people at local and national TESOL conventions who have said things like, "You were in Africa with me in 1964" or "We used the PD's in Ethiopia." It has given us a deep feeling of satisfaction to know that students of English in many parts of the world have found our book helpful.

To the Teacher

The purpose of *The PD's (Pronunciation Drills for Learners of English)* is to help ESL/EFL students internalize the systems of phonology and morphology of the language. To accomplish this purpose, presentation and practice materials are provided for all vowel, consonant, and stress phonemes, for the most frequently-occurring intonation patterns, and for the pronunciation of grammatical endings. The text also includes sections on the alphabet (pronunciation of names of letters and of common abbreviations and acronyms) and on sound-letter correspondences (common spelling patterns.)

In order to make most effective use of *The PD's*, the word *drill* should be taken seriously: that is, it should be understood that each lesson is intended to be intensive, fast-paced practice. At the end of a classwork session with any material from *The PD's*, students and teachers alike should feel that they have had a workout. Through use of *The PD's*, students should ideally be able to develop pronunciation of English which is close to that of a native speaker. At the very least, however, they should be able to acquire pronunciation which, though "foreign," will still be easily and immediately understood by native speakers.

The *PD's* text is designed with students at the low-intermediate through advanced proficiency levels in mind. It may be used at lower levels of instruction, however, with thorough introduction of lesson materials and procedures, plus clarification of any unfamiliar vocabulary items. The text alone is highly appropriate for teacher-directed class work, and if supplemented by the accompanying audio cassettes, is equally well-suited for use in language laboratories, learning center classes, or for individualized study programs. On the average, each PD will require from fifteen to twenty minutes of class time, although some are longer. More time will of course be necessary if any portion of a PD is repeated for extra practice or reinforcement.

Organization of Text Materials

In arranging the subject matter of *The PD's*, an atttempt has been made to introduce items in order of their importance—importance being determined by how frequently an item occurs in the language, coupled with the effect the item's mispronunciation would have on intelligibility. Accordingly, vowels are treated first (since every English syllable contains one), stress and intonation patterns are presented next (since every English word has a stress pattern and every English utterance has an intonation pattern), and consonants are treated last. There is also an internal order of items within each category:

PD's 1-5	the simple ("short") vowels: /i/, /e/, /æ/, /a/, /ɔ/, /ə/, /u/
PD's 7-12	the complex vowels ("long" vowels and diphthongs): /iy/, /ey/, /ay/, /oy/, /aw/, /ow/, /uw/, /yuw/
PD's 13, 14	"r-colored" vowels
PD 15	grammatical endings: pronoun forms, /S/, /ED/
PD's 16, 17	stress and intonation patterns
PD 18	/ð/ and /θ/ (treated first among consonants because of their high frequency of occurrence in common words—*the, this, that,* etc.
PD's 19, 20	the fricatives /s/ and /z/ and the stops /t/ and /d/ (treated next due to their prominent position in English morphophonology—i.e., in the pronunciation of /S/ and /ED/)
PD's 21-23	fricatives other than /s/ and /z/ (/f/, /v/, /h/), affricates /j/, /č/, and /š/, continuants /w/ and /y/
PD's 24-26	stops other than /t/ and /d/ (/p/, /b/, /k/, /g/), affricate /ž/
PD 27	/r/ and /l/

PD 28	the nasals /m/, /n/, and /ŋ/
PD's 29-36	consonant clusters
PD's 37-39	the alphabet and sound-letter correspondences (presented last because of reference to nearly all the preceding material)

Lesson Format

In *The PD's*, the basic lesson format is simple and clear-cut:

1. First, target items are presented in isolation. After a brief identification or description of the target sound or pattern, it is practiced in example words and sentences (or phrases, in the case of stress.)

2. After similar-sounding items have been individually introduced and practiced, they are treated in contrast exercises. In such exercises, much use is made of *minimal pairs* — two words differing in only one sound (e.g., *shop* and *chop* or *live* and *leave*.) When possible, minimal pair drills are also expanded to groups of three or even more words (e.g., *pit-pet-pat, tin-thin-sin, see-say-sigh-soy*.)

3. After groups of similar-sounding items have been worked with both in isolation and in contrast, they are further practiced by means of review sentences.

    NOTE: In *The PD's*, pronunciation variations are also identified. Two types of variation are treated: dialect differences (e.g., the pronunciation of the vowels in *pot* and *dog*) and common allophones (e.g., the sounds of /t/ in *tell, not, little, button*.)

Suggestions for Use of *The PD's*

Even though the individual characteristics of any group of students — class size, level of language-learning ability, whether the same or different native languages are spoken, how often and for how long the class meets, and so on — will determine exactly how *The PD's* should be used, the following guidelines should be kept in mind whenever *The PD's* is worked with:

1. Pronunciation problems students have or are likely to have must be identified. The *Pronunciation Problem Charts* (see below) are designed to facilitate this task.

2. Once pronunciation problems have been identified, drills concentrating on those problems should be selected for class work. The *Pronunciation Problem Charts* noted above also show which PD's are appropriate for specific pronunciation problems.

3. Classwork begins. In working through individual PD's, the teacher should pronounce each word or group of words, taking care to ensure that students can hear the sounds or patterns being worked with, and have students repeat. For best results, each PD should be drilled with individual students as well as with the class as a whole, and drillwork should be conducted in a lively, fast-paced manner.

4. Once individual PD's have been worked with in class, they should also be assigned for use in the language lab or learning center to provide further practice and reinforcement.

   NOTE: It should be made clear to students that the focus of *The PD's* is pronunciation, not vocabulary. Accordingly, any questions on the meaning of unfamiliar words should be resolved either before or after any work with the text is done.

Charts Included in *The PD's*

In addition to the text proper of *The PD's*, several charts have been included. These charts are intended to serve both as general reference tools and as aids in understanding and presenting the subject matter of the text. The charts are as follows:

1. *Symbol Conversion Chart*
   This chart (p. xiii) gives IPA – International Phonetic Association – equivalents for the symbols used in *The PD's* to refer to the sounds of English. For further clarification of the particular sounds being referred to, key words have also been provided to show each sound in context.

2. *Vowel Charts*
   Four vowel charts are provided. The first (p. xv) shows the relative positions of the tongue in the production of the simple vowels. In

this chart, tongue height and position (front, center, back of the mouth) are shown by means of a grid; presence or absence of lip rounding is also indicated. The second, third, and fourth vowel charts (p. xvi) show relative tongue positions for the complex vowels – those consisting of a simple vowel plus a glide. In Vowel Chart 2, the *y-glides* (those complex vowels in which the tongue moves upward and toward the front of the mouth from a simple vowel position) are shown. Vowel Chart 3 shows the *h-glides* (the complex vowels in which the glide is to a central position.) Vowel Chart 4 shows the *w-glides* (the complex vowels in which the glide is upward and toward the back of the mouth.)

3. *Consonant Articulation Chart*
   In this chart (p. xvii), the English consonant phonemes are classified according to place and manner of articulation; presence/absence of voicing is also indicated.

4. *Pronunciation Problem Charts*
   Two separate pronunciation problem charts, both of which are revisions and/or expansions of material from earlier editions of *The PD's*, are included. In the first (p. xviii), pronunciation problems that may be expected for all and most learners of English are listed. In the second (p. xix), probable pronunciation problems are listed according to students' native languages. In this chart 22 separate languages are treated.

   In both *Pronunciation Problem Charts,* areas of difficulty are identified and then followed by a list of PD's which are appropriate for work with the problems.

   NOTE: Because the *Pronunciation Problem Charts* are intended to be general reference tools as well as aids for use of *The PD's*, problem areas not specifically treated in the text are sometimes listed. In such cases, the particular PD's listed as appropriate for the problems may not deal with the area of difficulty extensively or exclusively.

5. *Vocabulary Used in PD's Lessons*
   Vocabulary items appearing in the example words, phrases, and sentences of *The PD's* are all of ultra high frequency, and have been garnered from the Bell Telephone, Thorndike, and authors' supplementary lists.

SYMBOL CONVERSION CHART

Key Words: Vowels	Symbols Used in the PD's[1]	IPA[2] Equivalent
h*ee*d	/ iy /	/ i /
h*i*d	/ i /	/ ɪ /
h*ay*ed	/ ey /	/ eɪ /
h*ea*d	/ e /	/ ɛ /
h*a*d	/ æ /	/ æ /
h*oy*den	/ ɨ /	/ ɨ /
H*u*d	/ ə /	/ ə /, / ʌ /
wh*o*'d	/ uw /	/ u /
h*oo*d	/ u /	/ ʊ /
h*oe*d	/ ow /	/ ou /
h*aw*ed	/ ɔ /	/ ɔ /
h*o*d	/ a /	/ ɑ /
h*i*de	/ ay /	/ ɑɪ /
h*o*yden	/ oy /	/ ɔɪ /
h*ow*'d	/ aw /	/ ɑʊ /

[1] The symbols used in this book are American Phonemic symbols, which are derived from the Trager-Smith analysis of English.

[2] "IPA" stands for International Phonetic Association.

Key Words: Consonants	Symbols Used in the PD's[1]	IPA[2] Equivalent
*b*ill	/ b /	/ b /
*ch*ill	/ č /	/ t ʃ /
*d*ill	/ d /	/ d /
*f*ill	/ f /	/ f /
*g*ill	/ g /	/ g /
*h*ill	/ h /	/ h /
*J*ill	/ j /	/ dʒ /
*k*ill	/ k /	/ k /
*L*il	/ l /	/ l /
*m*ill	/ m /	/ m /
*n*il	/ n /	/ n /
si*ng*	/ ŋ /	/ ŋ /
*p*ill	/ p /	/ p /
*r*ill	/ r /	/ r /
*s*ill	/ s /	/ s /
*sh*ill	/ š /	/ ʃ /
*t*ill	/ t /	/ t /
*th*igh	/ θ /	/ θ /
*th*y	/ ð /	/ ð /
*v*ine	/ v /	/ v /
*w*ine	/ w /	/ w /
*wh*ine[3]	/ hw / (/ w /)	/ ʍ / (/ w /)
*y*ou	/ y /	/ j /
*z*oo	/ z /	/ z /
vi*s*ion	/ ž /	/ ʒ /

[1] The symbols used in this book are American Phonemic symbols, which are derived from the Trager-Smith analysis of English.
[2] "IPA" stands for International Phonetic Association.
[3] The sound spelled with the letters *wh* is pronounced / hw / (/ ʍ /) in some dialects, and / w / in others.

ARTICULATION CHARTS

Vowel Nuclei

The following diagrams indicate the relative positions of the tongue in simple and complex vowels sounds. Diagram 1 illustrates simple vowel sounds. Diagrams 2, 3, and 4 demonstrate complex vowel sounds. Note that in complex vowel sounds, the tongue moves, or glides, from the simple position into another position. In the case of the y-glide (Diagram 2), the tongue moves upward and front; in the h-glide (Diagram 3), it moves toward the center; and in the w-glide (Diagram 4), it moves upward and backward.

Diagram 1: Simple Vowels

	Front *(unrounded)*	*Central* *(unrounded)*	*Back* *(rounded)*
High	i p*i*t	ɨ jud*g*es	u p*u*t
Mid	e p*e*t	ə j*u*dges	
Low	æ p*a*t	a p*o*t	ɔ (p*a*w)

Diagram 2: y-glide

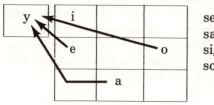

see /síy/
say /séy/
sigh /sáy/
soy /sóy/

Diagram 3: h-glide

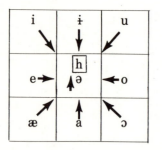

ear /íhr/
air /éhr/
(baa /bǽh/)
(bird /bɨhrd/)
(furred /fəhrd/)
bar /báhr/
sure /šúhr/
shore /šóhr/
(war /wɔhr/)

Diagram 4: w-glide

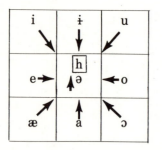

who /húw/
hoe /hów/
how /háw/ or /hæw/

Consonants

	Bi-labial		Labio-dental		Dental		Alveo-lar		Alveo-palatal		Velar		Glottal
	vl	vd	vl	vd	vl	vd	vl	vd	vl	vd	vl	vd	vl/vd
Stops	p	b					t	d			k	g	
Fricatives			f	v	θ	ð	s	z	š	ž			
Affricates									č	j			
Nasals	m						n					ŋ	
Resonants	w						l,(r)		y				h

Note: *vl*=voiceless; *vd*=voiced.

A SELECTED LIST OF PRONUNCIATION PROBLEMS
FOR ALL/MOST LEARNERS OF ENGLISH

Problems for	Areas of Difficulty	PD Numbers
all students	vowels	1-12
	stress and intonation	16, 17
	/ ð /, / θ /	18, 20
	/ r /	27
	vowels plus / r /	13, 14
	the alphabet, spelling patterns	37-39
most students	/ s / - / z /	19
	/ t / - / d /	20
	/ w / - / v /	21
	/ y / - / j /	22
	/ š / - / č /	23
	final / p /, / t /, / k /	19, 20, 24, 25
	/ l / - / r /	27
	/ ŋ /	28
	consonant clusters	29-32, 33-36

A SELECTED LIST OF PRONUNCIATION PROBLEMS ACCORDING TO STUDENTS' NATIVE LANGUAGES

Problems for Speakers of	Areas of Difficulty	PD Numbers
Arabic	/i/ - /e/ - /æ/	1
	/u/ - /ə/ - /a/	3-5
	/oy/	7, 8
	/i/ - /iy/, /e/ - /ey/	9
	/ow/	10, 11
	/u/ - /uw/	12
	/š/ - /j/ - /ž/	23, 26
	/p/	24
	/g/ - /j/	25
	/ŋ/	28
	consonant clusters	29-32, 33-36
Burmese	/i/ - /iy/, /e/ - /ey/	9
	/u/ - /uw/	12
	final /p/, /t/, /k/	19, 20, 24, 25
	/f/ - /v/	21
	/l/ - /r/	27
	final consonant clusters	33-36

Problems for Speakers of	Areas of Difficulty	PD Numbers
Chinese	vowels	1-14
	/ð/, /θ/	18
	/d/	19, 20
	/v/	21
	/b/	24
	/g/	25
	final consonants except /n/, /ŋ/	18-27, 33-36
	/h/ - /š/, /j/ - /ž/	22, 23
	/š/ - /č/	23
French	/ə/	3-5
	/oy/	7, 8
	/i/ - /iy/, /e/ - /ey/	9
	/u/ - /uw/	12
	/ð/, /θ/	18
	/t/ - /θ/ - /s/	20
	/h/	22
	/j/ - /ž/	22, 26

xx

Problems for Speakers of	Areas of Difficulty	PD Numbers
Navajo	/æ/, /ə/	1-5
	/æ/ - /a/	3, 4
	/ɔ/ - /a/	3, 4
	/a/ - /u/	5, 6
	/ay/, /oy/	7, 8
	/aw/, /ow/	10, 11
	/u/ - /uw/	12
	/θ/ - /ð/	18
	/f/ - /v/	21
	/p/ - /f/	21, 24
	/p/ - /b/, /b/ - /v/	24
	/t/ - /d/	19, 20
	/k/ - /g/	25
	/r/	27
	/m/ - /n/ - /ŋ/	28
	consonant clusters	29-32, 33-36
Persian (Farsi)	/i/ - /e/ - /æ/	1
	/a/ - /ɔ/	3
	/a/ - /ə/	3-5
	/i/ - /iy/, /e/ - /ey/	9
	/aw/ - /ow/	10
	/u/ - /uw/	12
	/ð/ - /θ/	18
	/θ/ - /s/	20
	/w/ - /v/	21
	/ŋ/ in medial position	28
	/s/ plus other consonants	29
	final consonant clusters	33-36

Problems for Speakers of	Areas of Difficulty	PD Numbers
Japanese	all vowels, particularly /iy/, /u(w)/	1-14, 16
	/ð/, /θ/	18
	/s/ - /š/, /z/ - /ž/	19, 26
	/t/ - /ts/ - /č/	19, 20, 23, 34
	/w/ - /v/	21
	/f/ - /h/	21, 22
	/š/ - /č/	23
	/l/ - /r/	27
	consonant clusters	29-32, 33-36
Korean	/i/ - /iy/, /e/ - /ey/	9
	/ow/ - /ɔh/	10, 11
	/u/ - /uw/	12
	all voiced consonants, particularly in final position	18-28
	/ð/, /θ/	18
	/p/, /t/, /č/, /k/ in medial position and before nasals	20, 23-25
	/l/ - /r/	27
	consonant clusters with /r/	33
Laotian	same as Thai, but not /l/ - /r/	

Problems for Speakers of	Areas of Difficulty	PD Numbers
Russian	/ə/ - /æ/	1
	/æ/ - /a/, /ə/ - /a/	3, 4
	/i/ - /iy/	9
	/ɔh/ - /ow/	11
	/u/ - /uw/	12
	/ð/, /θ/	18
	/w/, /v/	21
	/h/	22
	/r/	27
	/ŋ/	28
	voiced final consonants	18-28,33,35,36
Spanish	/æ/ - /a/, /æ/ - /ɔ/, /a/ - /ɔ/, /ə/ - /ɔ/	3, 4
	/u/ - /ə/	5, 6
	/i/ - /iy/, /e/ - /ey/	9
	/u/ - /uw/	12
	final consonants except /n, l, s, r/	18-28
	/s/ - /z/	19
	/d/ - /ð/	19, 20
	/θ/ - /s/	20
	/y/ - /j/	22
	/š/ - /č/	23
	/v/ - /w/	21
	/b/ - /v/	24
	final /m/, /n/, /ŋ/	28
	/s/ plus other consonants	29
	final consonant clusters	33-36

Problems for Speakers of	Areas of Difficulty	PD Numbers
Polish	/æ/	1-4
	/ə/	3-5
	/a/ - /æ/	3, 4
	long vowels and diphthongs, especially /i/ - /iy/, /uw/ - /yuw/	7-12
	unstressed syllables	16
	/ð/, /θ/	18
	/w/, /l/	21, 27
	/ŋ/, /ŋg/	28
Portuguese	final unstressed syllables	16
	/p/, /b/; /t/, /d/, /k/, /g/ in final position	19, 20, 24, 25, 33, 34
	/h/	22
	/č/ - /j/	23
	/r/	27
	/l/ in final position	27
	/n/, /ŋ/	28
	consonant clusters	29-32, 33-36

(For speakers of Brazilian Portuguese the following contrasts are a problem:

/t/ - /č(iy)/ and /d/ - /j(iy)/.)

PART I | *Vowels*

GROUP I | Vowels / i, e, æ /

PRONUNCIATION DRILL 1

1. THE VOWEL / i /

Words Frequently Used

Practice the following common words containing the "short *i* sound" /i/, as in *pit*.

pit	give	his	big
it	live	been	sing
is	15, 50	think	hit
in	16, 60	minute	million
him	will	sit	wish
with	which	women	Miss
this	did	busy	Mister
thing	didn't	business	Mrs.

Sentences

1. This is it.
2. Miss Mills thinks it's big.
3. Which children did it?
4. Is it his?

2. THE VOWEL / e /

Words Frequently Used

Practice the following common words containing the "short e sound" /e/, as in *pet*.

pet	when	F, L, M, N, S, X	Wednesday
get	weather	ten	February
let	dead	eleven	September
yes	sell	twelve	December
them	any	7, 17, 70	tell
men	many	well	then
says	very	better	again
said	yet	best	friend

Sentences

5. Let's get Ed a pen.
6. Many men said yes.
7. When did Ted send the letter?
8. The weather's better in September.

3. THE VOWEL / æ /

Words Frequently Used

Practice the following common words containing the "short a sound" /æ/, as in *pat*.

pat	back	man	can
at	that	ask	bad
as	catch	glad	last
has	Saturday	cab	laugh
have	perhaps	understand	half
had	matter	bag	class

NOTE: Some speakers of English have the sound /æ/ in words like "pat, back, catch" and the other words in the first and second columns but they may have different sounds, which we write /æh/ or /eh/, in words like "man, cab, bad" and in other words in the third and fourth columns. Other speakers of English have the same vowel sound in all the words above.

Sentences

9. Jack can't understand that.
10. That man ran after his hat.
11. Half the class has had it.
12. Has Dad had a nap?

4. VOWELS / i, e /

Words in Contrast

Concentrate only on the pronunciation of these words.

Now you will hear some pairs of words which differ only in having the "short *i* sound" /i/, as in *pit*, or the "short *e* sound" /e/, as in *pet*.

pit, pet	miss, mess	sit, set	pig, peg
pick, peck	rid, red	nick, neck	mitt, met
Sid, said	bit, bet	lid, led	pin, pen[1]
hid, head	knit, net	bliss, bless	since, sense[1]
din, den[1]	win, when	Jim, gem[1]	in, N[1]
string, strength	imminent, eminent[1]	did, dead	

Sentences

13. This weather is getting better.
14. Then again, I think it's best this way.
15. Let's get busy, men.

---

[1] Some speakers pronounce these words alike.

5. VOWELS / e, æ /

Words in Contrast

Now you will hear some pairs of words which differ only in having the "short *e* sound" /e/, as in *pet*, or the "short *a* sound" /æ/, as in *pat*.

pet, pat	mess, mass	dead, Dad	set, sat
peck, pack	neck, knack	beg, bag	bed, bad
said, sad	met, mat	net, gnat	led, lad
then[3], than	merry, marry[2]	very, vary[2]	M[3], am
lend[3], land	spend[3], spanned	N[3], an	

Sentences

16. Pass the jelly, Edna.
17. Get back exactly at midnight, Miss Smith.
18. Let's ask Dad's friends.

PRONUNCIATION DRILL 2

6. VOWELS / i, e, æ /

Words in Contrast

Now you will hear contrasts between the three sounds you have been practicing: /i/, /e/, and /æ/. There are conventional names for these three sounds. *Repeat them.*

Conventional Name	Sound	Examples
"the short *a* sound"	/ æ /	pat
"the short *e* sound"	/ e /	pet
"the short *i* sound"	/ i /	pit

---

[2]Some speakers pronounce both of these words the same way.

[3]Some speakers pronounce these words with /i/, not /e/.

6

Each of the following groups of words includes one word with one of the "short a sounds" /æ/ or /eh/, another word with "the short e sound" /e/, and a third word with "the short i sound" /i/.

pit, pet, pat	pat, pet, pit
sit, set, sat	set, sit, sat
lid, led, lad	led, lad, lid
nick, neck, knack	knack, nick, neck
knit, net, gnat	gnat, knit, net
bin, Ben, ban[4]	Ben, bin, ban[4]
mirror, merry, marry	miss, mess, mass
did, dead, Dad	mass, mess, miss
pick, peck, pack	dead, did, Dad
mitt, met, mat	pick, pack, peck
is, says, has	mat, met, mitt
pin, pen, pan[4]	has, says, is
dribble, rebel, rabble	in, N, an[4]

Review Sentences

Review sentences 1-18, which you have practiced. Sentences 19-22 have words with all the sounds you have been studying.

A. Sentences with / i /
　　1. This is it.
　　2. Miss Mills thinks it's big.
　　3. Which children did it?
　　4. Is it his?

B. Sentences with / e /
　　5. Let's get Ed a pen.
　　6. Many men said yes.
　　7. When did Ted send the letter?
　　8. The weather's better in September.

---

[4]Some speakers pronounce the first two words in these groups the same.

C. Sentences with / æ / or / eh /

   9. Jack can't understand that.
10. That man ran after his hat.
11. Half the class has had it.
12. Has Dad had a nap?

D. Sentences with / i / and / e /

13. This weather is getting better.
14. Then again, I think it's best this way.
15. Let's get busy, men.

E. Sentences with / e / and / æ /

16. Pass the jelly, Edna.
17. Get back exactly at midnight, Miss Smith.
18. Let's ask Dad's friends.

F. Sentences with / i /, / e /, and / æ /

19. Bill has seven children.
20. When did Ann tell him?
21. Has Ed been pretty busy?
22. The women met last Saturday.

GROUP II | Vowels / æ, a, ɔ, ə /

PRONUNCIATION DRILL 3

1. VOWELS / a, ɔ /

Words Frequently Used

There are many regional variations in the pronunciation of the "short o sounds." A large number of Americans use the /a/ vowel sound in the words in Column 1 and Column 2 below, and the /ɔ/ vowel sound in the words in Column 3 and Column 4. Imitate your teacher's pronunciation.

Practice the following common words containing the "short o sounds" /a/ and /ɔ/, as in *pot, dog.*

1	2	3	4
pot	hot	dog[1]	water[1]
not	dollar	chalk	call
got	October	gone	long
box	job	tall	lost
doctor	o'clock	often[1]	coffee[1]
a lot	watch	song	off[1]

[1]Some Americans use / a / in these words.

9

Sentences

1. The clock stopped.
2. It's not a lot.
3. Tom got the job in October.
4. The coffee's strong.
5. Ed lost his dog.
6. Is the song very long?

2. THE VOWEL / ə /

Words Frequently Used

Practice the following common words containing the "short *u* sound" /ə/, as in *putt* (a golf stroke).

putt	a cup	was²	double
up	the cup	from	trouble
us	some	Sunday	touch
but	of	Monday	mother
under	month	money	brother
sun	another	son	love
much	does	above	one
just	done	enough	won
one hundred	come	young	number

Sentences

7. The sun comes up at seven.
8. Mother loves the summer months.
9. Does Sunday come before Monday?
10. Hasn't Gus won enough money?

---

²Some Americans use /a/ in this word.

3. VOWELS / æ, a, ɔ /

Words in Contrast

Now you will hear some pairs of words which differ only in their vowel sounds: the "short *a* sound" /æ/, as in *lack*, or /eh/, as in *mass*; the "short *o* sound" /a/, as in *lock*, or /ɔ/, as in *moss*.

pat, pet	gnat, not	bass[3], boss	had, hod
map, mop	add, odd	bag, bog	sang, song
sad, sod	mass, moss	rat, rot	hag, hog
hat, hot	knack, knock	jab, job	passable, possible
lack, lock	cat, cot	nab, knob	tang, tong
lag, log	cab, cob	rang, wrong	impossible, impassable

Sentences

11. I want a *ham* sandwich—not a *hot* sandwich.
12. Has Ann got a job?
13. What had Jack's boss wanted?
14. Bob got back at one o' clock.

4. VOWELS / ə, a, ɔ /

Words in Contrast

Now you will hear some pairs of words which differ only in their vowel sounds: if the vowel letter is *u*, the sound is /ə/, as in *putt, but*; if the vowel letter is *o*, the sound is /a/ or /ɔ/, as in *pot* or *dog*.

pot, putt	lock, luck	hot, hut	rot, rut
moss, muss	boss, bus	dog, dug	long, lung
song, sung	wrong, rung	lost, lust	bossed, bust
scoff, scuff		cop, cup	

---

[3]"A kind of fish," / bæs /

Sentences

15. John's sorry, but he doesn't want to come.
16. The doctor does *not* come from Florida.
17. Bob mustn't touch the hundred-dollar watch.
18. Was John's *younger* brother in trouble?

PRONUNCIATION DRILL 4

5. VOWELS / æ, a, ɔ, ə /

Words in Contrast

Now you will hear some pairs of words which differ in their vowel sounds: the "short *a* sound" /æ/, as in *lack*, or /eh/, as in *mass*; the "short *o* sound" /a/, as in *pot*, or /ɔ/, as in *dog*; the "short *u* sound" /ə/, as in *putt*.

pat, pot, putt   blander, blonder, blunder
last, lost, lust   lack, lock, luck
sadden, sodden, sudden   gnat, knot, nut
mass, moss, muss   battle, bottle, rebuttal
stack, stock, stuck   bass, boss, bus
rang, wrong, rung   sang, song, sung

Sentences

19. When does Tom get back?
20. Tom gets back on Monday.
21. Does Kansas get as hot as it gets here?
22. Kansas got as hot as Washington last summer.

Review Sentences

Review the sentences which you practiced in PD 3 and PD 4.

A. Sentences with / a / or / ɔ /

    1. The clock stopped.
    2. It's not a lot.

3. Tom got the job in October.
4. The coffee's strong.
5. Ed lost his dog.
6. Is the song very long?

B. Sentences with / ə /

7. The sun comes up at seven.
8. Mother loves the summer months.
9. Does Sunday come before Monday?
10. Hasn't Gus won enough money?

C. Sentences with / æ / and / a / or / ɔ /

11. I want a *ham* sandwich – not a *hot* sandwich.
12. Has Ann got a job?
13. What had Jack's boss wanted?
14. Bob got back at one o'clock.

D. Sentences with / a / or / ɔ / and / ə /

15. John's sorry, but he doesn't want to come.
16. The doctor does *not* come from Florida.
17. Bob mustn't touch the hundred-dollar watch.
18. Was John's *younger* brother in trouble?

E. Sentences with / æ /, / a /, or / ɔ / and / ə /

19. When does Tom get back?
20. Tom gets back on Monday.
21. Does Kansas get as hot as it gets here?
22. Kansas got as hot as Washington last summer.

GROUP III | The Vowel / u /; Review of the Short Vowel Sounds

PRONUNCIATION DRILL 5

1. THE VOWEL / u /

Words Frequently Used

Practice the following common words containing the "short *oo* sound" /u/, as in *put*.

put	could	couldn't	push
good	should	shouldn't	pull
book	would	wouldn't	look
woman	wood	cook	took
foot	wool	woolen	full

Sentences

1. Would this be a good book?
2. He shouldn't have stood on that foot.
3. She took the book and put it away.
4. Look at that pretty woman.

2. VOWELS / u, ə /

Words in Contrast

Now you will hear some pairs of words which differ in their vowel sounds: the "short *u* sound" /ə/, as in *putt*; the "short *oo* sound" /u/, as in *put*.

putt, put	luck, look	cud, could	buck, book
tuck, took	stud, stood	crux, crooks	put, putt
look, luck	could, cud	book, buck	took, tuck
stood, stud	crooks, crux		

Sentences

5. She couldn't have stood the sight of blood.
6. Should one push it up or pull it down?
7. The woman wouldn't come up.
8. Good luck!

3. VOWELS / u, ə, a /

Words in Contrast

Now you will hear some groups of words which differ in their vowel sounds: the "short *oo* sound" /u/, as in *put*; the "short *u* sound" /ə/, as in *putt*; the "short *o* sound" /a/, as in *pot*.

Words with / u /:	put, good, look, could, book, shook
Words with / ə /:	putt, gun, luck, cud, buck, shuck
Words with / a /:	pot, god, lock, cod, bock, shock

pot, putt, put	could, cud, cod
god, good, gun	buck, bock, book
look, lock, luck	shuck, shook, shock

Sentences

9. The book was *not* good.
10. Would you look at Bobby's foot, Mother?

11. The woman put the books back in the box.
12. The parking lot was full.

4. THE SHORT VOWEL SOUNDS

Review

Here is a complete list of the short vowel sounds in one type of standard American speech. Listen when the speaker says, "say the short *i* sound, as in *pit*," then repeat.

Conventional Name	Phonemic Symbol	Key Words
the short *i* sound	/ i /	pit
the short *e* sound	/ e /	pet
the short *a* sound	/ æ /, / eh /	pat, man
the short *o* sound	/ a/, / ɔ /	pot, dog
the short *u* sound	/ ə /	putt, but
the short *oo* sound	/ u /	put, good

Be sure you can pronounce the following groups of key words correctly.

pat, pet, pit   pot, putt, put
pet, pit, pat   put, pot, putt
pet, pat, pot   pit, pet, pat, pot, putt, put
pat, pot, putt   put, putt, pot, pat, pet, pit
pot, putt, pat

Be sure you can pronounce the following groups of words correctly.

miss, mess, mass   din, Dan, Don
mass, moss, muss   Dan, den, din, Don, dun
miss, mass, muss   pill, pal, pull
mess, moss, mass   but, bat, bottle
mass, mess, miss   bat, bet, bit, bottle, but
miss, moss, muss   back, buck, book
                        back, beck, bicker, buck, book

PRONUNCIATION DRILL 6

5. VOWELS / ɔh, ah /

Words Frequently Used

Practice the following common words containing the "*aw* sound" /ɔh/, as in *saw*.

saw	call	because	brought
Shaw	fall	applause	thought
straw	small	caught	walk
awful	Paul	ought	daughter
all	pause	bought	cough

Turn back to PD 3 and review the words in Columns 3 and 4, and the remarks in the paragraph above. In the words "dog, long, off," and in other words spelled with *o*, many Americans do not use the short vowel sound /ɔ/: they use a similar vowel sound of longer duration, written here as /ɔh/. This is the "*aw* sound" which you practiced in the words listed above, "saw, call," and so forth.

There are a great many regional variations in the pronunciation of the "short *o* sounds" and the "*aw* sound." Imitate your teacher's pronunciation.

Sentences

13. I thought I saw Paul.
14. Has Mr. Hall taught law?
15. All Shaw thought of was applause.
16. We ought to walk and talk together.

6. VOWELS / ɔh, ah /

Words in Contrast

Now you will hear some pairs of words which differ in their vowel sounds: one word has the "*aw* sound" /ɔh/, as in *saw*; the other word has the "short *o* sound" /a/ or /ɔ/, as in *pot, dog*[1].

---

[1]Some speakers pronounce most or all of these pairs the same.

coffer, cougher	nod, gnawed	cod, cawed	odd, awed
cot, caught	Poll, Paul	tot, taught	not, naught
knotty, naughty	rot, wrought	chock, chalk	stock, stalk
yon, yawn	Oz, awes	clod, clawed	Don, dawn

The /ah/ sound in contrast with /a/ and /ɔh/

A great many speakers of English in the Eastern United States have a vowel sound that is like /a/, but is of longer duration. The phonemic writing for this sound is /ah/ and the most usual spellings are -a and -ah at the end of a word, and the a in -alm.

ah!	Ma	palm
Shah	spa	psalm
Pa	calm	father

/a/ - /ah/ contrasts

| bomb, balm | insomnia, psalm | bother, father |
| comma, calmer | pod, Pa'd | |

/ah/ - /ɔh/ contrasts

| ah!, awe | Ma, maw | Pa, pawn |
| Shah, Shaw | spa, spawn | Pa's, pause |

If your teacher says words like *bomb* and *balm* alike, imitate his pronunciation. Both types of pronunciation are correct.

7. VOWELS / u, ə, a, ɔh/

Review Sentences

Review sentences 1-16, which you studied in PD 5 and in PD 6. Practice sentences 17-20, which have words with all the sounds you have been studying.

A. Sentences with / u /
1. Would this be a good book?
2. He shouldn't have stood on that foot.
3. She took the book and put it away.
4. Look at that pretty woman.

B. Sentences with / ə / and / u /

    5. She couldn't have stood the sight of blood.
    6. Should one push it up or pull it down?
    7. The woman wouldn't come up.
    8. Good luck!

C. Sentences with / u / and / ə / and / a /

    9. The book was *not* good.
  10. Would you look at Bobby's foot, Mother?
  11. The woman put the books back in the box.
  12. The parking lot was full.

D. Sentences with / ɔh /

  13. I thought I saw Paul.
  14. Has Mr. Hall taught law?
  15. All Shaw thought of was applause.
  16. We ought to walk and talk together.

E. Sentences with / u, ə, a, ɔh /

  17. Would Paul and Don be fond of one another?
  18. The song was good.
  19. Joe Shaw should call up his father.
  20. What book would Dr. Davis suggest?

GROUP IV | Complex Vowels / iy, ey, ay, oy /

PRONUNCIATION DRILL 7

1. THE COMPLEX VOWEL / iy /

Words Frequently Used

Practice the following common words containing the "long *e* sound" /iy/, as in *see*.

see	he	week	maybe
B, C, D, E	she	meet	need
G, P, T, V, Z	we	evening	complete
three	these	please	keep
be	mean	seem	people
me	believe	the[1]	leave

---

[1]pronounced /oiy/.

Sentences

1. Keep these three for me, please.
2. He sees me three evenings a week.
3. These people seem to believe me.

2. THE COMPLEX VOWEL / ey /

Words Frequently Used

Practice the following common words with the "long *a* sound" /ey/, as in *say*.

say	place	ate	make
A, J, K, H	wait	they	maybe
8, 18, 80	weight	April	rain
May	same	eight	stay
may	name	take	lane
way	vacation	neighbor	pay

Sentences

4. They say they'll take a vacation.
5. Eight days in April, and eighteen in May.
6. The rain in Spain stays mainly in the plain.

3. THE COMPLEX VOWEL / ay /

Words Frequently Used

Practice the following common words containing the "long *i* sound" /ay/, as in *sigh*.

sigh	like	Friday	night
I, Y	my	July	eye
5	mine	all right	fine
9, 19, 90	time	write	by
hi	child	why	buy
high	might	nice	good-bye

Sentences

7. I'd like to buy a nylon tie.
8. My child likes ice cream.
9. Why arrive at five to nine?
10. I'll try to find time by Friday.

4. THE COMPLEX VOWEL / oy /

Words Frequently Used

Practice the following common words containing the "*oy* sound" /oy/, as in *boy*.

boy	noise	joy	enjoy
choice	noisy	join	boil
toy	coin	Hoyt	avoid
annoy	oil	Freud	oyster

Sentences

11. Roy's enjoying his toys.
12. The boys are rather noisy.

THE NAMES OF THE SOUNDS / iy, ey, ay, oy /

Review the names of the sounds you have been studying in PD 7. There are conventional names for the sounds /iy/ and /ey/ and /ay/. We will call /oy/ the "*oy* sound" since it is almost always spelled *oy* as in *boy*, or *oi* as in *choice* or *noisy*.

Say the conventional names of the other complex vowels, and the key words.

	Phonemic Symbol	*Conventional Name*	*Key Words*
1.	/ey/	the long *a* sound	lake, say
2.	/iy/	the long *e* sound	leak, see
3.	/ay/	the long *i* sound	like, sigh

PRONUNCIATION DRILL 8

5. THE COMPLEX VOWELS / iy, ey, ay, oy /

Words in Contrast

Now you will hear some pairs of words which differ in their vowel sounds: one word has the "long *e* sound" /iy/, as in *see*; the other word has the "long *a* sound" /ey/, as in *say*.

Pete, pate	seat, sate	read, raid	Mead, made
E, A	grease, Grace	lease, lace	seen, sane
mean, main	reek, rake	seek, sake	deem, dame
seem, same	fade, feed	swayed, Swede	slave, sleeve

Sentences

13. We eat steak once a week these days.
14. She always takes the street car from the station.
15. The "ABCs" means "the alphabet."

6. COMPLEX VOWELS / ay, oy /

Words in Contrast

Now you will hear some pairs of words which differ in their vowel sounds: one word has the "long *i* sound" /ay/, as in *sigh*; the other word has the "*oy* sound" /oy/, as in *boy*.

try, T	buys, boys	fried, Freud	rise, Roy's
sigh, soy	rye, Roy	I'll, oil	tie, toy
file, foil	kind, coined	pies, poise	vied, void
line, loin	vice, voice	quite, quoit	trite, Detroit
implies, employs		implied, employed	

Sentences
16. I like boiled rice and soy sauce.
17. I sang "What kind of a noise annoys an oyster."

7. COMPLEX VOWELS / iy, ey, ay, oy /

Words in Contrast

Now you will hear some groups of words which differ in their vowel sounds. Each word in the group has one of the four following sounds: the "long *e* sound" /iy/, as in *see*; the "long *a* sound" /ey/, as in *say*; the "long *i* sound" /ay/, as in *sigh*; the "*oy* sound" /oy/, as in *soy*.

see, say, sigh, soy	A, E, I
tree, tray, try, Troy	grain, green, groin
style, stale	toil, tile, tail, teal
poi, pie, pay, pea	B, bay, by, boy
join, Jane, Jean	steel, stale, style
soy, sigh, see, say	peas, pays, poise
Troy, try, tree, tray	cane, keen, coin
	see, say, soy, sigh

Sentences

18. He's my baby boy.
19. Has he tried to read James Joyce?
20. My neighbors seem to be nice people.

8. COMPLEX VOWELS / iy, ey, ay, oy /

Review Sentences

Review the sentences you practiced in PD 7 and PD 8.

A. Sentences with / iy /
  1. Keep these three for me, please.
  2. He sees me three evenings a week.
  3. These people seem to believe me.

B. Sentences with / ey /
  4. They say they'll take a vacation.
  5. Eight days in April, and eighteen in May.
  6. The rain in Spain stays mainly in the plain.

C. Sentences with / ay /

    7. I'd like to buy a nylon tie.
    8. My child likes ice cream.
    9. Why arrive at five to nine?
   10. I'll try to find time by Friday.

D. Sentences with / oy /

  11. Roy's enjoying his toys.
  12. The boys are rather noisy.

E. Sentences with / iy, ey, ay, oy /

  13. We eat steak once a week these days.
  14. She always takes the street car from the station.
  15. The "ABCs" means "the alphabet."
  16. I like boiled rice and soy sauce.
  17. I sang "What kind of a noise annoys an oyster."
  18. He's my baby boy.
  19. Has he tried to read James Joyce?
  20. My neighbors seem to be nice people.

GROUP V | Vowels / i, iy, e, ey /

PRONUNCIATION DRILL 9

1. VOWELS / i, iy /

Words in Contrast

This is a very important section. Now you will hear some pairs of words which differ in their vowel sounds. The first word has the "short *i* sound" /i/, as in *live*; the second word has the "long *e* sound" /iy/, as in *leave*.

pit, Pete	live, leave	rid, read	sin, seen
sick, seek	sit, seat	chip, cheap	gyp, jeep
slip, sleep	ship, sheep	lip, leap	fit, feet
grits, greets	mitt, meet	hit, heat	dip, deep

Sentences

1. Potato chips are cheap.
2. Did they fit his feet?
3. Please sit in this seat.
4. I leave the house where I live at five o'clock.
5. Did he say "living" or "leaving"?

2. VOWELS / iy, i /

Words in Contrast

Now you will hear some pairs of words which differ in their vowel sounds. The first word has the "long e sound" /iy/, as in *leave*; the second word has the "short i sound" /i/, as in *live*.

leave, live	he'd, hid	steal, still	meal, mill
cheek, chicken	ease, is	we'll, will	deep, dip
eat, it	tease, 'tis	feel, fill	bean, bin
lead, lid	he's, his	kneel, nil	these, this
deed, did	Gene, gin	green, grin	peat, pit

Sentences

6. He's been eating his meals at the mill.
7. Is the steel strike still on?
8. Which of these women did he see?
9. She didn't meet the three children — she missed them.
10. Is it easy?

3. VOWELS / e, ey /

Words in Contrast

This is a very important section. Now you will hear some pairs of words which differ in their vowel sounds. The first word has the "short e sound" /e/, as in *let*; the second word has the "long a sound" /ey/, as in *late*.

pet, pate	let, late	debt, date	red, raid
bet, bait	met, mate	pen, pain	den, Dane
led, laid	wet, wait	get, gate	Ed, aid
Ned, neighed	pepper, paper	wreck, rake	ebb, Abe
fed, fade	bread, braid	west, waste	special, spatial

Sentences

1. They get ten days' vacation.
12. On what date was the debt paid?

13. Your weight is greater when you're wet.
14. Did they say "pepper" or "paper"?

4. VOWELS / ey, e /

Words in Contrast

Now you will hear some pairs of words which differ in their vowel sounds. The first word has the "long *a* sound" /ey/, as in *late*; the second word has the "short *e* sound" /e/, as in *let*.

late, let	wage, wedge	age, edge	wade, wed
stayed, stead	phase, fez	taste, test	chased, chest
Yale, yell	sale, sell	lace, less	tale, tell
James, gems	spatial, special	quail, quell	waste, west
main, men		aches, X	

Sentences

15. They went to bed late.
16. Jane said they'd already met her.
17. Did she take the dress with less lace?
18. They stayed instead of us.

5. VOWELS / i, iy, e, ey /

Review Sentences

Review sentences 1-18, which you have practiced in PD 9. Practice sentences 19-22, which have words with all the sounds you have been studying.

A. Sentences with / i / and / iy /
  1. Potato chips are cheap.
  2. Did they fit his feet?
  3. Please sit in this seat.
  4. I leave the house where I live at five o'clock.
  5. Did he say "living" or "leaving"?

6. He's been eating his meals at the mill.
7. Is the steel strike still on?
8. Which of these women did he see?
9. She didn't meet the three children – she missed them.
10. Is it easy?

B. Sentences with / e / and / ey /

11. They get ten days' vacation.
12. On what date was the debt paid?
13. Your weight is greater when you're wet.
14. Did they say "pepper" or "paper"?
15. They went to bed late.
16. Jane said they'd already met her.
17. Did she take the dress with less lace?
18. They stayed instead of us.

C. Sentences with / i, iy, e, ey /

19. Will we stay? Yes, we'll stay.
20. They said we might get rain this evening.
21. Did they feel better?
22. They feel better than they felt yesterday.

GROUP VI | Complex Vowels / aw, ow, uw /

PRONUNCIATION DRILL 10

1. THE COMPLEX VOWEL / aw /

Words Frequently Used

Practice the following common words with the "*ou* sound" /aw/, as in *house*.

house	power	south	mouth
out	down	cow	proud
hour	doubt	towel	around
our	now	found	ounce
noun	town	sound	pound
about	mouse	thousand	amount
how	cloudy	ground	round

Sentences

1. "Around" and "about" are not nouns.
2. I doubt that he's downtown.
3. How much is a pound of ground round? (steak)

NOTE: Many Americans say /æw/ instead of /aw/, and find the latter sound artificial.

2. THE COMPLEX VOWEL / ow /

Words Frequently Used

Practice the following common words containing the "long o sound" /ow/, as in *know*.

know	go	close	Ohio
O	so	clothes	show
no	old	home	both
nose	don't	whole	Oklahoma
coat	won't	telephone	told
November	over	moment	only
hold	those	chose	though

Sentences

4. Rose and Joan don't know yet.
5. Oh, did Joe go home?
6. Both those cars are pretty old.

3. THE COMPLEX VOWEL / uw /

Words Frequently Used

Practice the following common words containing the "long oo sound" /uw/, as in *two*.

too	soon	prove	shoe
two	who	proof	through
to	whom	choose	soup
do	whose	spoon	group
afternoon	food	loose	tooth
you	move	lose	blue

Sentences

7. Do you have a loose tooth?
8. I'm moving to another room this afternoon.
9. Whose group do you belong to?

4. THE COMPLEX VOWEL / uw /

Words Frequently Used

The words listed below, like the words in 3, have the /uw/ sound, but when it is spelled with the letter *u*, it is conventionally named the "long *u* sound." The letter *u* also represents the sounds /yuw/, and the conditions under which the /y/ sound is present before the /uw/ are explained below in the *Note*, and illustrated in 5.

Practice the following common words containing the "long *u* sound" /uw/, as in *rule*, or /yuw/, as in *use, few*.

rule	knew	excuse me	suit
Q, U	news	music	juice
June	beauty	fruit	use (n.)
July	beautiful	review	use (v.)
Tuesday	usually	human	used to

Sentences

10. We used to have quite a few arguments about music.
11. Ruth had some fruit juice in her room.
12. Who will tell the students the news?

NOTE: Read This with Your Teacher's Help:

Many Americans pronounce "long *u*" as follows:
/yuw/ = initially and after /b, f, m, p, v/ and /k, g, h/;
/uw/ = after the other consonant sounds /č, d, j, l, n, r, s, š, θ, z/.

Many other speakers of English, particularly in the American South, have two types of "long *u*" distributed as follows:
/yuw/ = Initially, after /b, f, m, p, v/, /k, g, h/, /d, l, n, s, t/;
/uw/ = after the remaining consonant sounds /č, j, r, š, θ, z/.

This means that words like *Tuesday, new,* and *suit* are pronounced with either the /uw/ sound or the /yuw/ sound, depending on the region.

Some other speakers have a sound we write /ɨw/ after all the consonant sounds in all words with the "long *u*" sound. These regional variations are all acceptable. Imitate your teacher's pronunciation.

5. THE SOUNDS / uw, yuw /

Words in Contrast

Now you will practice some words which have the sound /uw/: either the "long *oo* sound," as in *too*, or the type of "long *u* sound," as in *rule*; and the sound /yuw/, the other type of "long *u* sound," as in *use* and *few*.

In the words in Column 1 below, all speakers use /uw/; in the words in Column 2, speakers of English use /uw/ or /yuw/, according to the part of the country they come from; in the words in Column 3, all speakers use /yuw/.

	1		2		3
	/uw/		/(y)uw/		/yuw/
oo, o	*u, ew*[1]		*u, ew*[2]		*u, ew*[3]
too	chew	Tuesday	use	music
do	June	due	pupil	excuse
soon	juice	new	beauty	argue
who	rule	enthusiasm	few	human
zoo	true	student	review	usually

It follows that some speakers, but not all, have a contrast in the following few pairs of words:

do, due   gnu, knew   too, Tuesday   loot, lute

All speakers have a contrast in pairs like the following:

who, hue	whose, hues	who'll, Hugh'll	whom, Hume
coo, Q	fool, fuel	pooh, pew	coot, cute
	moo, mew	mood, mewed	

---

[1] after /č, j, r/
[2] after /d, l, n, s, t, θ/
[3] initially, and after other consonants

34

The important thing to remember when you have a word with a "long *u* sound" is this: pronounce "long *u*" as /yuw/ at the beginning of a word and after *b, c, f, g, h, m, p,* and *v.*

6. COMPLEX VOWELS / aw, ow /

Words in Contrast

Now you will hear some pairs of words which differ in their vowel sounds: the first word has the "*ou* sound" /aw/, as in *house*; the second word has the "long *o* sound" /ow/, as in *know*.

sow,[4] so	noun, known	now, no	now's, knows
how, hoe	blouse, blows	loud, load	scowled, scold
	rouse, rose	out, oat	

PRONUNCIATION DRILL 11

7. VOWELS / ow, ɔh /

Words in Contrast

Now you will hear some pairs of words which differ in their vowel sounds: the first has the "long *o* sound" /ow/, as in *know*; the second word has the "*aw* sound" /ɔh/, as in *saw*.

so, saw	coat, call	Joe, jaw	phone, fawn
coat, caught	owe, awe	droll, drawl	scroll, scrawl
toll, tall	boat, bought	oaf, off	hole, hall
low, law	cold, called	goes, gauze	close, clause
woke, walk	ode, awed	coast, cost	row, raw
choke, chalk	mode, Maude	loan, lawn	slow, slaw
oat, ought		pose, paws	

---

[4]"female swine," /saw/

35

Sentences

13. A local phone call costs ten cents.
14. Now's the time to show us how.
15. Do cows cause tuberculosis?
16. Now, Paul, drive downtown slowly.

8. VOWELS / aw, ɔh /

Words in Contrast

The "ou sound" /aw/, as in *house*, and the "aw sound" /ɔh/, as in *saw*, are not at all similar in sound. Occasionally, however, there is confusion between /aw/ and /ɔh/, partly because of the complexity of the English spelling system.

Now you will hear some pairs of words which differ only in their vowel sounds: the first word has the "ou sound" /aw/ as in *house*; the second word has the "aw sound" /ɔh/, as in *saw*.

sow, saw	cloud, clawed	fowl, fall
allow, a law	bout, bought	cow, caw
mouse, moss	loud, laud	cows, cause
tout, taught	souse[5], sauce	pound, pawned
brown, brawn	down, dawn	row[6], raw
sows, saws	louse, loss	howl, hall
found, fawned		

9. VOWELS / aw, ow, uw /

Words in Contrast

Say the conventional names of the complex vowels /aw, ow, uw/, and then the key words.

---

[5]Some Americans say /sawz/ instead of /saws/.

[6]"noisy disturbance or quarrel," /raw/.

Phonemic Symbol	*Conventional Name*	*Key Words*
1. /aw/	the *ou* sound	house, now
2. /ow/	the long *o* sound	hope, coat, no
3. /uw/	the long *oo* sound	soon, too, do
4. /uw/ or /yuw/	the long *u* sound	rule, use, few

We have used the symbol /(y)uw/ as a cover symbol to mean the sound /uw/ whether or not it was preceded by the /y/ sound, and whether it was represented in the spelling by *oo*, by *u*, or by some other letters.

Now you will hear some groups of words which differ only in their vowel sounds: one of each group of three words has the "*ou* sound" /aw/, as in *house*; another word has the "long *o* sound" /ow/, as in *hope*; the other word has the "long *u* sound" /(y)uw/, as in *rule* or *use*.

new, no, now	mow[7], moo, mow[8]	sues, sews, sows
whose, hose, house (v.)	road, rude, rowed	who, hoe, how
sue, so, sow		ruse, rose, rouse

Sentences

17. Who drove you downtown?
18. I doubt that you know the rules.
19. Do you know how to get to school?
20. "Food" and "nose" are nouns.

PRONUNCIATION DRILL 12

10. VOWELS / u, uw /

Words in Contrast

Now you will hear some pairs of words which differ in their vowel sounds: the first word has the "short *oo* sound" /u/, as in *put* and *good*; the second word has the "long *oo* sound" /uw/, as in *too*.

---

[7]"cut grass with a sickle or machine," /mow/

[8]"a pile of hay; a storage place for hay," /maw/.

pull, pool	full, fool	stood, stewed	wood, wooed
look, Luke	could, cooed	should, shoed	hood, who'd
book, rebuke	soot, suit	foot, refute	put, impute
Toots, toots	look, leukemia	wooden, wound	

You have already studied the "short *oo* sound" /u/. Although this sound does not occur in very many words, the words in which it *does* occur are very frequently used.

put	foot	wood	stood
good	could	wool	push
book	should	took	pull
woman	would	look	full

Sentences

21. Would some good food put you in a good mood?
22. Ruth should move to a *good* rooming house.

11. VOWELS / aw, ow, uw, (y)uw /

Review Sentences

Review the sentences you practiced in PD 10, 11, and 12.

A. Sentences with / aw /
    1. "Around" and "about" are not nouns.
    2. I doubt that he's downtown.
    3. How much is a pound of ground round? (steak)

B. Sentences with / ow /
    4. Rose and Joan don't know yet.
    5. Oh, did Joe go home?
    6. Both those cars are pretty old.

C. Sentences with / uw /
    7. Do you have a loose tooth?
    8. I'm moving to another room this afternoon.
    9. Whose group do you belong to?

D. Sentences with / (y)uw /

    10. We used to have quite a few arguments about music.
    11. Ruth had some fruit juice in her room.
    12. Who will tell the students the news?

E. Sentences with / aw, ow, uw, (y)uw /

    13. A local phone call costs ten cents.
    14. Now's the time to show us how.
    15. Do cows cause tuberculosis?
    16. Now, Paul, drive downtown slowly.
    17. Who drove you downtown?
    18. I doubt that you know the rules.
    19. Do you know how to get to school?
    20. "Food" and "nose" are nouns.
    21. Would some good food put you in a good mood?
    22. Ruth should move to a *good* rooming house.

GROUP VII | Vowels before /r/

PRONUNCIATION DRILL 13

1. THE SOUND /ihr/

Words Frequently Used

Practice the following common words containing the "long *e-r* sound" /ihr/, as in *ear*.

ear	tear[1]	rear	Shakespeare
hear	dear	merely	cheerful
here	year	fear	superior
near	weary	interfere	beer

NOTE: There are many dialects of English that linguists call "r-less" because they do not have /r/ except *before vowels*. Such dialects are Southern British (Received Standard), and parts of New York City, New England, and the coastal Southern U.S. Imitate your teacher's pronunciation, keeping in mind that it may not match the transcription given here.

---

[1]"liquid from the eye," /tihr/.

41

Sentences

1. Keep the earphones nearer, dear.
2. Shakespeare's *King Lear* showed here last year.

2. THE SOUND / ehr /

Words Frequently Used

Practice the following common words containing the "long *a-r* sound"
/ehr/, as in *air*.

air	their	fare	various
hair	there	fair	chair
care	where	Mary	spare
stairs	wear	tear (v.)	Claire

Sentences

3. Where are the stairs?
4. Careful! Don't tear it on that chair.

3. THE SOUND / ohr /

Words Frequently Used

Practice the following common words containing the "*o-r* sound" /ohr/,
as in *four*.

1	*2*	*3*	*4*
four	door	or	horse
fourteen	floor	for	war
pour	store	fork	warm
more	pork	morning	short

Sentences

5. This store has four floors.
6. George just bought a four-door Ford.

NOTE: Many speakers have the vowel /ɔh/ in all the words in columns 1, 2, 3, and 4. Some other speakers have that vowel in the words in Columns 1 and 2, and the "short *o* sound" /ɔ/, as in *boss,* in the words in Columns 3 and 4 and similar words. Such speakers have a contrast between *horse* and *hoarse, morning* and *mourning, war* and *wore.* Imitate your teacher's pronunciation.

There is considerable difference in pronunciation of these words in various parts of the United States. Some have /oh/ in Columns 1 and 2, and /ɔh/ in Columns 3 and 4; other speakers may have /oh/ in all these words, or /ɔh/ in all.

4. THE SOUND /uhr/

Words Frequently Used

Practice the following common words with the "long *u-r* sound" /uhr/, as in *sure.*

sure	poor	Moore	tour
cure	you're	curious	tourist
pure	your	jury	insurance

Sentences

7. Tourists should be sure to drink pure water.
8. Be sure to check your life insurance.

NOTE: Many speakers pronounce *your, poor,* and other words spelled with *oo* and *u,* with the same vowel sound which you practiced in the previous section on the sound /ohr/. They are often the same speakers who use two different vowels in words like *store* and *horse.* Imitate your teacher's pronunciation.

5. THE SOUND /a(h)r/

Words Frequently Used

Practice the following common words containing the "*a-r* sound" /ar, ahr/, as in *are.*

	1	*2*	*3*	*4*
	are	far	yard	tomorrow
	R	heart	bar	sorry
	March	hard	barred	orange
	large	army	parking	Florida
	car	par	farm	Oregon

A speaker from the New York City area says /ar/ or /ahr/ in all these words. Some speakers say /ar/ or /ɔr/ in the words in Column 4, like *sorry*. New England speech characteristically has /æ(h)r/ for /a(h)r/, as in *park the car*. Imitate your teacher's pronunciation.

Sentences

9. Park the car in the back yard.
10. Florida and Oregon are pretty far apart.

6. THE SOUND /ə(h)r/

Words Frequently Used

Practice the following common words containing the "*ur* sound" /ər, əhr/, as in *were*.

were	learn	worse	skirt
thirteen	person	worst	shirt
thirty	sir	first	hurry
Thursday	girl	early	verb
her	nervous	work	thorough
worry	burn	world	earth

Sentences

11. Were the little girls with her, sir?
12. Learn the first thirty verbs thoroughly.

44

7. VOWELS BEFORE /r/

Words in Contrast

The vowel sounds before *r* which you have studied in 1-6 of Group VII are reviewed below. The contrasts are those made in one variety of standard Northeastern speech. Remember that there are many correct ways of pronouncing American English, and that there are very many differences, from region to region, in the pronunciation of the simple and complex vowels before *r*.

Listen, then repeat. First repeat each column (1, 2, etc.), then repeat each line (1, 2, etc.).

	1 /ihr/	2 /ehr/	3 /ohr/	4 /uhr/	5 /a(h)r/	6 /ə(h)r/
1.	ear	air	oar	– –	are	err[2]
2.	peer	pair	pour	poor	par	purr
3.	mere	mare	more	moor	mar	myrrh
4.	sear	Sarah	sore	– –	Saar	sir
5.	tear (n.)	tear (v.)	tore	tour	tar	turn

Sentences

13. The girls were wearing scarves and earmuffs and their warmest coats.
14. We're parking your car over there.

PRONUNCIATION DRILL 14

8. SOUNDS / ər, ihr /

Words in Contrast

Now you will hear some pairs of words which differ in their vowel sounds: the first word has the "*ur* sound" /ər, əhr/, as in *were*; the second word has the "long *e-r* sound" /ihr/, as in *ear*.

---

[2]Also pronounced /e(h)r/.

her, here	purse, pierce	bird, beard	fur, fear
worry, weary	err, ear	sir, seer	word, weird
purr, peer	myrrh, mere	burr, beer	stir, steer
were, we're		shirr, sheer	

Sentences

15. We're always here on Thursday, sir.
16. Herbert's girl friend lives near here.
17. Is this your first year at Burlington University?

9. SOUNDS /ər, ehr /

Words in Contrast

Now you will hear some pairs of words which differ in their vowel sounds: the first word has the "*ur* sound" /ər, əhr/, as in *were*; the second word has the "long *a-r* sound" /ehr/, as in *air*.

err, air	stir, stair	her, hair	whir, where
were, wear	stirred, stared	purr, pair	fur, fare
hurry, hairy	cur, care	burr, bear	

Sentences

18. We're wearing their shirts.
19. Is it thirty years since we were there?
20. Here's where we were working.

10.   SOUNDS / ə(h)r, a(h)r, o(h)r/

Words in Contrast

Now you will hear some pairs of words which differ only in their vowel sound: the first word has the "*ar* sound" /ar, ahr/, as in *are*; the second word has the "*ur* sound" /ər, əhr/, as in *were*.

are, err	far, fur	star, stir	hard, heard
heart, hurt	bard, bird	carve, curve	

Now you will hear some other pairs of words: the first word has the "*or* sound" /or, ohr/, as in *pore*; the second word has the "*ur* sound" /ər, əhr/, as in *were*.

pour, purr	sport, spurt	warm, worm	store, stir
hoard, heard	oar, err	for, fur	coarse, curse
born, burn	torn, turn	war, were	

Sentences

21. "Are" and "were" are parts of the verb *to be*.
22. Are the girls learning any more German?
23. George and Charles were warmly dressed.

11.   VOWELS BEFORE /r/

Review Sentences

Review the sentences which you studied in PD 13 and 14.

A. Sentences with / ihr /
   1. Keep the earphones nearer, dear.
   2. Shakespeare's *King Lear* showed here last year.

B. Sentences with / ehr /
   3. Where are the stairs?
   4. Careful! Don't tear it on that chair.

C. Sentences with / o(h)r /
   5. This store has four floors.
   6. George just bought a four-door Ford.

D. Sentences with / uhr /
   7. Tourists should be sure to drink pure water.
   8. Be sure to check your life insurance.

E. Sentences with / a(h)r /
   9. Park the car in the back yard.
   10. Florida and Oregon are pretty far apart.

F. Sentences with / ə(h)r /

11. Were the little girls with her, sir?
12. Learn the first thirty verbs thoroughly.

G. Sentences with vowels before / r /

13. The girls were wearing scarves and earmuffs and their warmest coats.
14. We're parking your car over there.

H. Sentences with / ər, ihr /

15. We're always here on Thursday, sir.
16. Herbert's girl friend lives near here.
17. Is this your first year at Burlington University?

I. Sentences with / ər, ihr, ehr /

18. We're wearing their shirts.
19. Is it thirty years since we were there?
20. Here's where we were working.

J. Sentences with / ər, o(h)r, a(h)r /

21. "Are" and "were" are parts of the verb *to be*.
22. Are the girls learning any more German?
23. George and Charles were warmly dressed.

| # Grammatical Endings, Stress, Intonation

PRONUNCIATION DRILL 15

1. GRAMMATICAL ENDINGS

English has very few grammatical suffixes. Adverbs, conjunctions, prepositions, and exclamations do not have grammatical suffixes. Some adjectives, but not all adjectives, have suffixes for comparison: *-er* /ər/ for the comparative degree, and *-est* /ɪst/ for the superlative degree — rich, richer, richest; poor, poorer, poorest. Nouns and verbs may have grammatical endings, and pronouns have different forms and endings.

Pronouns

All pronouns have a subject form, an object form, and two possessive forms. Listen, then repeat.

Subject Form	Object Form	1st Possessive Form	2nd Possessive Form
I	me	my	mine
you	you	your	yours
he	him	his	his
she	her	her	hers
it	it	its	
who	who(m)	whose	whose
we	us	our	ours
they	them	their	theirs

Here are sentences which use all four forms of the pronouns.

1. I put my money on the table, and John asked me if it was mine.
2. You put your money on the table, and John asked you if it was yours.
3. She put her money on the table, and John asked her if it was hers.
4. We put our money on the table, and John asked us if it was ours.
5. They put their money on the table, and John asked them if it was theirs.

Nouns

Most nouns have a singular form, a plural form, a singular possessive form, and a plural possessive form.

Singular	Plural	Singular Possessive	Plural Possessive
cat	cats	cat's	cats'
dog	dogs	dog's	dogs'
judge	judges	judge's	judges'
wife	wives	wife's	wives'
man	men	man's	men's

The plural ending s, and the possessive endings 's and s' of the same noun are all pronounced alike. The *noun suffixes -s, -'s,* and *-s'* are pronounced in one of three different ways (/s, ɨz, z/) depending on the last sound of the noun. For example:

the s in *cats, cat's, cats'* is pronounced /s/;
the s in *dogs, dog's, dogs'* is pronounced /z/;
the s in *judges, judge's, judges'* is pronounced /ɨz/.

50

Noun Suffixes

The pronunciation of the noun suffixes (-s, -'s, -s') is determined by the last sound of the noun. In Column 1 below, the sounds followed by /s/ are listed, together with key words; in Column 2 below, the sounds followed by /ɨz/ are listed, together with key words; in Column 3 below, the sounds followed by /z/ are listed, together with key words.

	Column 1		*Column 2*	
	/s/		/ɨz/	
	after p, pe, t, te,		after s, se, ce,	
	k, ke, f, fe,		z, ze, x, (t)ch,	
	ph, gh, th, etc.		(d)ge	
/p/	maps, tapes, stamps		/s/	uses (n.), places, taxes
/t/	seats, lights, satellites		/z/	uses (v.), Liz's, quizzes
/k/	checks, headaches, snakes		/š/	ashes, wishes
/f/	roofs, staff's, photographs, coughs, Ralph's		/ž/	garages
/θ/	months, laths		/č/	matches, Rich's, niches
			/j/	judges', edges

Column 3

/z/

after vowel spellings, and
b, be, d, de, g, gue,
ve, the, m, me, n, ne,
ng, l, le, r, re

/V/	ties, Joe's	/m/	names, claims
/b/	clubs, Abe's	/n/	fans, Anne's
/d/	Ed's, cathodes	/ŋ/	songs, kings'
/g/	eggs, plagues	/l/	smiles, walls
/v/	wives', waves	/r/	car's, ears
/ð/	lathes, clothes		

Verbs

The verb "to be" has these forms: *be, am, is, are, being, been, was, were.* All other verbs have a maximum of five different forms. (Tenses and moods are really phrases of 2 to 4 words, one of which words is one of the five different forms below.)

1. Common form	2. 3rd singular form	3. Present participle form	4. Past form	5. Past participle
walk	walks	walking	walked	walked
sing	sings	singing	sang	sung
beat	beats	beating	beat	beaten
lie	lies	lying	lay	lain
wish	wishes	wishing	wished	wished
knit	knits	knitting	knitted	knitted

Practice the pronunciation of the *verb suffix* for the 3rd singular form, used after *he, she, it,* and singular *nouns* and *pronouns* as in *he says, she has, it does, who is, the man sings.* The pronunciation of the *verb suffix -s, -es* is identical with the pronunciation of the *noun suffixes* which you studied previously. It is pronounced one of three different ways (with /s, ɨz, z/) depending on the last sound of the common form of the verb. For example:

the *s* in *walks, beats, knits* is pronounced /s/;
the *s* in *sings, lies* is pronounced /z/;
the *es* in *wishes* is pronounced /ɨz/.

Verb Suffixes

The pronunciation of the "third singular verb suffix," spelled *-s* or *-es,* is always /s, z, ɨz/ added to the *common form* of the verb.

There are only four verbs in English which do not follow this rule.

I am - he is
I do - he does
I say - he says
I have - he has

All the other regular verbs are in three classes: Column 1 has verbs with final sounds followed by /s/; Column 2 has verbs with final sounds followed by /ɨz/, and Column 3 has verbs with final sounds followed by /z/, all with key words. Repeat the key words.

Column 1
/s/

after p, pe, t, te,
k, ke, f, fe,
ph, gh, th, etc.

/p/	helps, stops, wipes
/t/	wants, fits, rotates
/k/	works, takes, checks
/f/	laughs, coughs, rebuffs
/θ/	froths

Column 2
/ɨz/

after s, se, ce
z, ze, sh, x, (t)ch,
(d)ge

/s/	notices, increases, kisses
/z/	uses, oozes, buzzes
/š/	rushes, cashes
/ž/	rouges
/č/	reaches, itches
/j/	changes, obliges

Column 3
/z/

after vowel spellings, and
b, be, d, de, g, gue,
ve, the, m, me, n, ne,
ng, l, le, r, re

/V/	ties, knows, sees	/m/	seems, times
/b/	grabs	/n/	means, learns
/d/	attends, decides	/ŋ/	longs for, sings
/g/	drags, begs	/l/	smiles, calls
/v/	lives, arrives	/r/	hears, cares, remembers
/ð/	bathes, breathes		

Verbs Ending in -ed

Many verbs called "regular verbs" have *-ed* as their past ending, or *-d* if the verb already has an *e* as its last letter. This ending is pronounced /t/ or /d/ *in the same syllable with the verb,* unless the last letters of the verb are *t, d, te,* or *de.*

As in *verb suffixes,* the regular verbs fall into three classes: Column 1 has verbs with final sounds followed by /ɨd/, Column 2 has verbs with final sounds followed by /t/, Column 3 has verbs with final sounds followed by /d/. Say the key words.

Column 1		Column 2	
/ɨd/		/t/	
after t, te, d, de		after p, pe, t(ch), k, ke, f, fe, ph, gh, th, s, se, x, sh	
/t/	wanted, fitted, seated, waited, expected, delighted, rested, rotated, completed	/p/	helped, stopped, wiped
		/č/	reached, itched
		/k/	checked, worked, asked, talked, smoked, baked
/d/	needed, attended, added, crowded, decided, faded	/f/	laughed, coughed, rebuffed
		/θ/	frothed
		/s/	noticed, increased, kissed, dressed, taxed
		/š/	rushed, cashed

Column 3
/d/

after vowel spellings and
all other voiced consonants:
b, be, (d)ge, g, gue,
v, the, m, me, n, ne,
ng, l, le, r, re

/V/	tied, allowed	/m/	named, claimed
/b/	grabbed	/n/	learned, cleaned
/j/	judged	/ŋ/	longed for
/g/	dragged, begged	/l/	smiled, called
/v/	lived, arrived	/r/	heard, cared, remembered
/ð/	bathed, breathed	/ž/	rouged[1]

---

[1]Some speakers pronounce this word with /j/, not /ž/.

PRONUNCIATION DRILL 16

2. STRESS

Stress Patterns

Stress means "loudness." In English, there are four grades of stress. Often, a small difference in the stress pattern makes a large difference in the meaning.

Here are the names of the four grades of stress, and two ways to represent them:

Names of Stress	Dot Symbol	Accent Symbol
Weak (quiet)	•	˘
Tertiary (loud)	•	ˋ
Secondary (louder)	•	˄
Primary (loudest)	●	´

Here is a well-known example of two different stress patterns on the same phrase:

● •
1. White House
   The president lives in the Whìte Hòuse.

   • ●
2. white house
   The family lives in the whîte hóuse.

● •   • ●
Whìte Hòuse   whîte hóuse

Stress Patterns on Words

Below are the five most frequent stress patterns. They consist of Primary Stresses and Weak Stresses. Notice the occurrence of the vowels /ə/ and /ɨ/ in weak syllables.

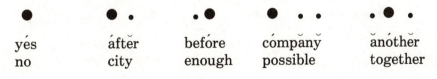

●	● •	• ●	● • •	• ● •
yés	áftĕr	befóre	cómpănў	ănóthĕr
no	city	enough	possible	together

man	little	believe	usual	consider
good	saying	result	happily	tomorrow
fast	added	above	gathering	believing

Here are some other stress patterns consisting of one Primary Stress and one or more Weak Stresses:

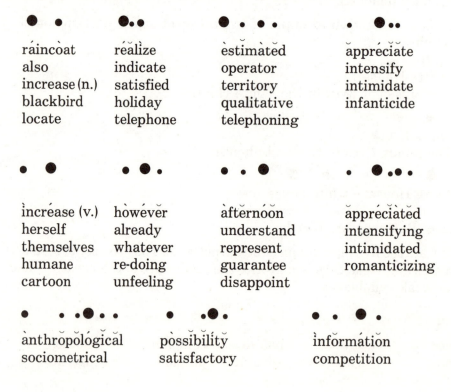

• ●..	• ●..	• ●.. •	● . . . •
América	expérience	immédiately	pássionately
American	especially	imaginative	practicable
Republican	material	conditionally	amicable

Other Stress Patterns on Words

Earlier in this Pronunciation Drill, you practiced stress patterns consisting of Primary and Weak Stresses. Many words have one Primary Stess, one Tertiary Stress, and some Weak Stresses:

● •	●..	● . . .	• ●..
ráincoat	réalize	éstimated	appréciate
also	indicate	operator	intensify
increase (n.)	satisfied	territory	intimidate
blackbird	holiday	qualitative	infanticide
locate	telephone	telephoning	

• ●	• ● •	• . ●	• ●.● •
incréase (v.)	howéver	áfternóon	appréciàted
herself	already	understand	intensifying
themselves	whatever	represent	intimidated
humane	re-doing	guarantee	romanticizing
cartoon	unfeeling	disappoint	

• . .●..	• .●.	• . ● .
ànthropólogical	pòssibility	informátion
sociometrical	satisfactory	competition

regimentational   unconditional   education
                                           operation
                                           Democratic

•..●.   ● ..●...
specifications   anthropologically
mathematician   sociometrically
semicoherent

There are a few pairs of words in English which are alike except for the stress pattern. They have different meanings. Say the words below:

August - august   import (v.) - import (n.)   permit (v.) - permit (n.)

Stress Contrasts

Now you will hear some pairs of words which differ in having one Primary Stress, or a Primary Stress and a Weak Stress.

pop, poppy	might, mighty	itch, itchy	rock, rocky
Bob, Bobby	shade, shady	edge, edgy	bag, baggy
leaf, leafy	pith, pithy	sis, sissy	bush, bushy
move, movie	rose, rosy	room, roomy	rain, rainy
tang, tangy	Bill, Billy	star, starry	cough, coffee
sit, city	red, ready	laid, lady	hill, hilly
doll, dolly	pat, patty	part, party	putt, putty
dot, Dotty	boot, booty	stone, stony	wind, windy
droop, droopy	tab, tabby	Tom, Tommy	pen, penny

Sentences

1. Chicago is called the Windy City.
2. Billy, your coffee is ready.

Stress Patterns on Phrases

Some of the stress patterns which appear with phrases consist of Primary Stresses, Tertiary Stresses, and Weak Stresses. Listen to the phrases below, classified by their stress patterns, then repeat:

● ●	● ●	● ●
ă dáy	ăt hóme	tŏ dó
an egg	in time	to say
the men	to bed	to think

●.	●.
dó it	ísn't
tell 'im	couldn't
say it	didn't

● ●	● ●	● ●	● ●
pùt ón	hòw múch	a loàf of breád	càll úp
take off	quite fast	a lot of money	bring up
get on	has seen	ice cream	He's here.
get off	was done	old maid	It is.

● ●	● ●	● ●
póst òffice	cóffee brèak	tíe pìn
phone call	swimming pool	pie tin
shaving cream	ball game	girl friend
White House	fish net	ice cream

Other Stress Patterns on Phrases

Many stress patterns on phrases include the Secondary Stress. Every phrase includes only one Primary Stress and may have Secondary, Tertiary, and Weak Stresses.

Secondary+Primary is the usual pattern for adjective+noun, verb+adverb, and, in short sentences, noun+verb.

Adjective+Noun	*Verb+Adverb*	*Noun+Verb*
● ●	● ●	● ●
bìg bóy	wâlk fást	Jòhn's góne.
beautiful woman	sing well	Dick sings.
white cap	come now	Marian decided.

four paws	eat quickly	Cows moo.
black car	jump off	Dogs bark.
white dress	come to	Horses neigh.

Stress Patterns in Contrast

The same phrase has one meaning if its stress pattern is Secondary+Primary (˄ + ˊ), and a different meaning if its stress pattern includes a Tertiary Stress. Listen to the following phrases in contrast, then repeat:

Secondary+Primary	*Primary+Tertiary*	*Tertiary+Primary*

1. old maid
   (former servant)

2. Paul Jones
   (a man's name)

3. red cap
   (hat which is red)

4. blue bird
   (a bird which is blue)

5. black board
   (a piece of wood that is black)

6. four-foot steps
   (steps which are 4 feet high)

7. four paws
   (all 4 feet of an animal)

8. long island
   (an island which is long)

3a. redcap
   (porter)

4a. bluebird
   (certain species of bird)

5a. blackboard
   (writing surface in a classroom)

6a. four footsteps
   (sound or impression of feet)

7a. forepaws
   (the 2 front feet of an animal)

1a. old maid
   (spinster)

2a. Paul Jones
   (name of a dance)

8a. Long Island
   (name of an island off New York)

9. white house (a house which is white)	9a. White House (President's house)	
10. iced cream (cream which is iced)	10a. ice cream (dessert)	10b. ice cream (dessert)

Sentences

1. Is the Whíte Hoùse | really a whíte hóuse?
2. Lòng Ísland | really is a lóng ísland.
3. A rédcàp | used to wear a rêd cáp.
4. A bláckbòard | is seldom a bláck bóard.
5. A blúebìrd | is not the only blùe bírd.

PRONUNCIATION DRILL 17

3. INTONATION

Intonation is the tune of what we say, or the way our voices go up and down as we speak. In English there are four significant levels of pitch. Pitch means the highness or lowness of the voice. We can represent the four pitches in English in this way:

```
4 ═══════════════════════
3 ───────────────────────
2 ───────────────────────
1 ═══════════════════════
```

The lowest pitch (represented on line 1) is usually used at the end of sentences. A higher pitch (represented on line 2) is usually used at the beginning of sentences: in a long sentence, most of the words will be spoken on this pitch. A still higher pitch (represented on line 3) is also used. The strongest stress usually occurs with the highest pitch in a sentence, but this is not always true. The highest pitch of all (represented on line 4) is not used as often as the other three. It has a special connotation, such as emphasis, surprise, or emotion.

The most frequent intonation pattern in English is the 2-3-1 pattern. That is, the sentence begins on pitch two, goes up to pitch three, and goes down to pitch one at the end. This rise or fall, to or toward another pitch, may occur in one syllable. We call this a glide. Glides usually occur with the strongest stress.

Below are some examples of sentences having the 2-3-1 intonation pattern.

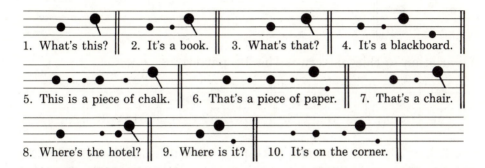

A variation of the 2-3-1 pattern is the 3-1 pattern. This is used in short sentences and phrases, usually when the strongest stress occurs on the first syllable. Below are some examples of phrases and sentences having the 3-1 pattern.

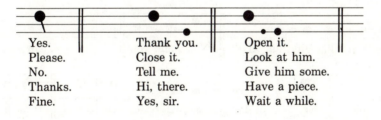

Practice counting, using the 3-1 intonation.

The 2-3-2 intonation pattern is also frequently used in English. Below are some sentences and phrases with the 2-3-2 pattern.

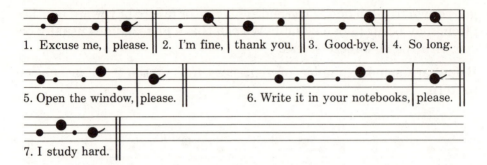

1. Excuse me, please. 2. I'm fine, thank you. 3. Good-bye. 4. So long.

5. Open the window, please. 6. Write it in your notebooks, please.

7. I study hard.

A variation of this pattern is the 3-2 pattern.

8. Fine, thanks. 9. Hi, Dick. 10. That's right. 11. O. K.

The 2-3, or rising intonation, pattern is used in English, usually for a question that can be answered with *yes* or *no*. Below are some examples.

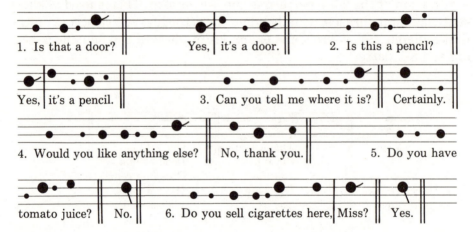

1. Is that a door? Yes, it's a door. 2. Is this a pencil?

Yes, it's a pencil. 3. Can you tell me where it is? Certainly.

4. Would you like anything else? No, thank you. 5. Do you have

tomato juice? No. 6. Do you sell cigarettes here, Miss? Yes.

A rising intonation turns a statement into a question.

If you say ![He bought it yesterday.] , you are making a statement.

He bought it yesterday.

If you say 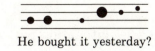, you are asking a question.

He bought it yesterday?

Do NOT use the rising intonation with a statement construction unless you mean to ask a question.

Uses of the Intonation Patterns

Falling Intonation: 2-3-1, 3-1, 2-3-2

a. Statements:

2   3 1   3   1   2   3   2
It's raining.   John's here.   I'm fine, thanks.

b. Commands:

2   31   3 1   2   3   2
Close the door.   Tell me.   Open the window, please.

c. Questions Except Those To Be Answered by Yes or No:

2   3   1   3   1   2 3 2
What time is it?   Who's coming?   Who is it?

Rising Intonation: 2-3

a. Questions Which Can Be Answered by Yes or No:

2   3   2   3
Is it time for dinner?   Can you speak English?

2   3
Do you have a pencil?

b. Questions Constructed Like a Statement:

2   3   2   3
She went to school today?   You went to the movies?

2   3
This bus goes to town?

Review

Below are some questions with the 2-3-1 intonation pattern.

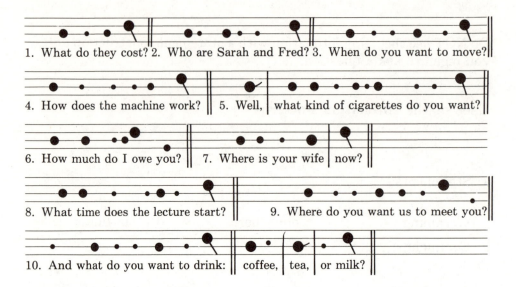

1. What do they cost? 2. Who are Sarah and Fred? 3. When do you want to move?

4. How does the machine work? ‖ 5. Well, what kind of cigarettes do you want?

6. How much do I owe you? ‖ 7. Where is your wife now?

8. What time does the lecture start? ‖ 9. Where do you want us to meet you?

10. And what do you want to drink: ‖ coffee, tea, or milk?

Below are some statements with the 2-3-1 intonation pattern.

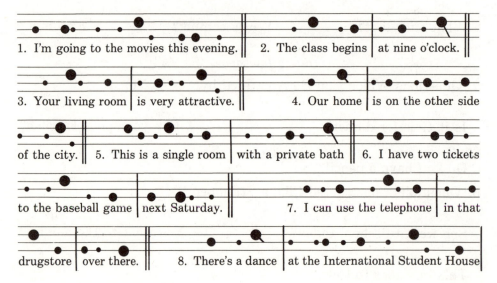

1. I'm going to the movies this evening. ‖ 2. The class begins at nine o'clock.

3. Your living room is very attractive. ‖ 4. Our home is on the other side

of the city. ‖ 5. This is a single room with a private bath ‖ 6. I have two tickets

to the baseball game next Saturday. ‖ 7. I can use the telephone in that

drugstore over there. ‖ 8. There's a dance at the International Student House

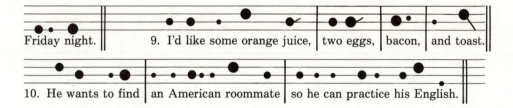

Friday night. 9. I'd like some orange juice, | two eggs, | bacon, | and toast.

10. He wants to find | an American roommate | so he can practice his English.

PART II | *Consonants*

GROUP IX | Consonants / θ, ð, s, z, t, d /

PRONUNCIATION DRILL 18

1. CONSONANTS / θ, ð /

Words Frequently Used

In English, the letters *th* represent two different sounds: the "voiced *th* sound" as in *they*, and the "voiceless *th* sound," as in *think*. Both sounds are made by putting the tongue between the teeth, but the sound written /θ/ is voiceless, like /f/, and the sound written /ð/ is voiced, like /v/.

The "voiced *th* sound" is the first sound in a very small number of English words (around twenty), but many of these words are used with very great frequency. The common words are given in the first three columns (1, 2, 3) below. Words in the fourth column (4) are archaic or rare.

Practice the following common words with the "voiced *th* sound" /ð/, as in *they*.

	1	2	3	4
	the	they	then	thou
	this	them	than	thee
	that	their	thus	thy
	these	theirs	though	thine
	those	there	therefore	thither, thence

The voiced *th* sound is also found in the middle of words, and at the end of words where it is regularly spelled *-the* (exceptions: *smooth* and sometimes *with*).

mother	another	northern	either
father	rather	southern	neither
brother	bother	smoother	bather
weather	whether	smooth(e)	bathe

Sentences

1. My brothers did that themselves.
2. Their car is better than this one.
3. Are they going there some other day, Mother?
4. Although these southern cities have better weather, I'd rather visit the northern ones.

2. THE CONSONANT /θ/

Words Frequently Used

Practice the following common words containing the "voiceless *th* sound" /θ/, as in *think*.

think	thirteen	month	theater
thought	thirty	mouth	anything
thanks	third	south	everything
thorough	thousand	healthy	nothing
thumb	thing	wealthy	mathematical

The voiceless *th* sound is the last sound in a number of nouns.

warm - warmth	long - length (n.)
heal - health (n.)	breathe - breath (n.)
strong - strength (n.)	wide - width (n.)
deep - depth (n.)	

The suffix -*th* is used to make the adjective forms of the numbers, beginning with 4.

fourth	eighth	twelfth	twentieth
fifth	ninth	thirteenth	fiftieth
sixth	tenth	fourteenth	hundredth
seventh	eleventh	fifteenth	thousandth

Sentences

5. Let's thank her for the theater tickets.
6. "Thick" and "thin" mean opposite things.
7. Does the month of June have thirty days or thirty-one?
8. I thought I'd go south, not north.

3. CONSONANTS / θ, ð /

Words in Contrast

Now you will hear some pairs of words which differ in having the "voiceless *th* sound" /θ/, as in *think*, or the "voiced *th* sound" /ð/, as in *they*. The first word has /θ/; the second word has /ð/.

thigh, thy	teeth, teethe
wrath, rather	wreath, wreathe
mouth, mouthe	lath, lather
sooth, soothe	ether, either
zither, dither	sheath, sheathing

Sentences

9. This is the third toothbrush I've lost this month.
10. The baby's teething, so her mouth is rather sore.
11. Congratulations! You're the thousandth person to visit this theater.

12. Would you rather have gas or ether?

13. Neither gas nor ether—no anesthetics, thanks.

14. They have to think this thing through.

4. CONSONANTS / θ, ð /

Review Sentences

Review the sentences you practiced in PD 18.

A. Sentences with / ð /

    1. My brothers did that themselves.

    2. Their car is better than this one.

    3. Are they going there some other day, Mother?

    4. Although these southern cities have better weather, I'd rather visit the northern ones.

B. Sentences with / θ /

    5. Let's thank her for the theater tickets.

    6. "Thick" and "thin" mean opposite things.

    7. Does the month of June have thirty days or thirty-one?

    8. I thought I'd go south, not north.

C. Sentences with / θ / and / ð /

    9. This is the third toothbrush I've lost this month.

    10. The baby's teething, so her mouth is rather sore.

    11. Congratulations! You're the thousandth person to visit this theater.

    12. Would you rather have gas or ether?

    13. Neither gas nor ether—no anesthetics, thanks.

    14. They have to think this thing through.

PRONUNCIATION DRILL 19

5. CONSONANTS / s, z, t, d /

Words Frequently Used

In English, the "s sound" and the "z sound" are made by touching the sides of the tongue to the tooth ridge, and letting a stream of air come out over the middle of the tongue, which is curved. The opening at the middle of the tongue is small. The "s sound" is voiceless like /f/, and the "z sound" is voiced like /v/.

Practice the following common words containing the "s sound" /s/, as in *say*.

say	sister	S	this
see	Mr. (Mister)	Miss	us
C	professor	nice	listen
6, 16, 60	person	place	use (n.)
7, 17, 70	possible	worse	less

Sentences

1. "See" and "say" begin with *s*.
2. Miss Ross said yes.
3. Did your sister send this to us?
4. Is Sunday the second of September?

6. THE CONSONANT / z /

Words Frequently Used

Practice the following common words containing the "z sound" /z/, as in *zero*.

zero	Tuesday	crazy	was	easy
Z	Wednesday	Missouri	is	business
zoo	Thursday	dessert	has	as
thousand	busy	his	does	says

Sentences

5. Please excuse me.
6. He always goes to the zoo on Thursdays.
7. Is his home in Arizona?
8. A thousand has three zeros.

7. CONSONANTS / s, z /

Words in Contrast

Now you will hear some pairs of words which differ in having the "s sound" /s/, as in *sink*, or the "z sound" /z/, as in *zinc*. The first word has /s/; the second word has /z/.

sue, zoo	see, Z	sip, zip	ice, eyes
bus, buzz	hiss, his	niece, knees	piece, peas
cease, sees	decrease, decrees	close, close[1]	scion, Zion
dice, dies	price, prize	loose, lose	face, phase
sink, zinc			

Sentences

9. She goes to the zoo to see the animals.
10. Sara's your sister, isn't she?
11. His suit is the same as this one.
12. What size dress does Susie wear?

8. CONSONANTS / t, d /

Words Frequently Used

In English, the "t sound" and the "d sound" are made by the tip of the tongue touching the ridge just above and behind the upper teeth. The tongue does not touch the teeth. The "t sound" is voiceless like /f/, and the "d sound" is voiced like /v/.

Practice the following common words containing the "t sound" /t/, as in *tell, little, button.*

1	*2*	*3*	*4*
tell	not	little	button
T	get	better	mountain
to, too, two	cigarette	butter	bitten

---

[1]adjective, verb

74

12, 10	wet	later	written
talk	sit	eating	satin
tall	let	sitting	gotten

In the middle of a word (see Column 3) *t* sounds like *d* in the speech of many Americans. Listen, then repeat.

little	put it away	eighty
butter	latter	later
better	eating	bottom

Before /n/ in a weak syllable (see Column 4), *t* has still another sound. Listen, then repeat.

button	kitten	rotten
mountain	bitten	satin
fountain	written	

The suffix *-ed* after certain sounds is pronounced like *t*. Listen, then repeat.

helped	laughed
stooped	promised
packed	missed

Sentences

13. Try to talk in English all the time.
14. Can you tell me the time?
15. You'd better put a little butter on it.
16. Is a better bottle of wine pretty expensive?
17. It was written by Mr. Sutton.
18. Don't button the bottom button of your jacket.

9. THE CONSONANT / d /

Words Frequently Used

Remember that in English, the "d sound" is made by the tip of the tongue touching the ridge just above and behind the upper teeth. The tongue does not touch the teeth. The "d sound" is voiced like /v/.

Practice the following common words containing the "d sound" /d/, as in day.

day	don't	good	hold
D	dollar	bad	old
do	doing	could	hand
did	didn't	would	mind
done	idea	should	need
doctor	anybody	had	road
December	condition	find	hard

The suffix -ed after certain sounds is pronounced /d/. Listen, then repeat.

lived	pulled
agreed	remembered
bathed	

Sentences

19. A *good* doctor wouldn't do that.
20. What day in December did he come?
21. I couldn't find the dollar I had.
22. Ted had a good idea, didn't he?

PRONUNCIATION DRILL 20

10. CONSONANTS / t, d, s, z, θ, ð /

Words in Contrast

Now you will hear some pairs of words which differ in having the "*t* sound"

/t/, as in *ten,* or the "*d* sound" /d/, as in *den.* The first word has /t/; the second word has /d/.

tin, din	tie, die	two, do	tee, D
tip, dip	town, down	tome, dome	time, dime
tell, dell	wait, wade	latter, ladder	bitter, bidder
matter, madder	satin, sadden	written, ridden	height, hide
bet, bed	wrote, rode	bit, bid	late, laid
rot, rod	mate, maid	plate, played	light, lied

Sentences

23. Tell Dotty to do it.
24. Today is cold, isn't it?
25. Ted said he couldn't stay for dessert.
26. Don't you know the word "date"?

11. CONSONANTS / t, θ, s /

Words in Contrast

Now you will hear some groups of words which differ in having the "*t* sound" /t/, as in *tin;* the "*th* sound" /θ/, as in *thin;* or the "*s* sound" /s/, as in *sin.* The first word has /t/, the second word has /θ/, and the third word has /s/.

tin, thin, sin	taught, thought, sought	tank, thank, sank
tick, thick, sick	tinker, thinker, sinker	true, threw, sue
taw, thaw, saw	teem, theme, seem	

Sentences

27. Thanks for the cigarettes, Miss Thorp.
28. Sixteen times two equals thirty-two.
29. The best theater tickets cost from three to six dollars.
30. Thursday and Sunday were hot, but today is nice.

12. CONSONANTS / d, ð, z /

Words in Contrast

Now you will hear some groups of the words which differ in having the "*d* sound" /d/, as in *den*; the "voiced *th* sound" /ð/, as in *then*; and the "*z* sound" /z/, as in *Zen*. The first word has /d/, the second word has /ð/, and the third word has /z/.

den, then, Zen
breeding, breathing, breezing
teed, teethe, tease
D, thee, Z
seed, seethe, seize

dine, thine, resign
ladder, lather, lazar
bayed, bathe, baize
lied, lithe, lies

Sentences

31. Their ideas are always good.
32. They have Wednesday off, don't they?
33. These old roads are in bad condition.
34. Is his father a doctor?

13. CONSONANTS / s, z, t, d, θ, ð /

Review Sentences

Review the sentences you practiced in PD 19 and 20.

A. Sentences with / s /

    1. "See" and "say" begin with *s*.
    2. Miss Ross said yes.
    3. Did your sister send this to us?
    4. Is Sunday the second of September?

B. Sentences with / z /

    5. Please excuse me.
    6. He always goes to the zoo on Thursdays.
    7. Is his home in Arizona?
    8. A thousand has three zeros.

C. Sentences with / s / and / z /

    9. She goes to the zoo to see the animals.
10. Sara's your sister, isn't she?
11. His suit is the same as this one.
12. What size dress does Susie wear?

D. Sentences with / t /

13. Try to talk in English all the time.
14. Can you tell me the time?
15. You'd better put a little butter on it.
16. Is a better bottle of wine pretty expensive?
17. It was written by Mr. Sutton.
18. Don't button the bottom button of your jacket.

E. Sentences with / d /

19. A *good* doctor wouldn't do that.
20. What day in December did he come?
21. I couldn't find the dollar I had.
22. Ted had a good idea, didn't he?

F. Sentences with / t / and / d /

23. Tell Dotty to do it.
24. Today is cold, isn't it?
25. Ted said he couldn't stay for dessert.
26. Don't you know the word "date"?

G. Sentences with / t /, / θ /, and / s /

27. Thanks for the cigarettes, Miss Thorp.
28. Sixteen times two equals thirty-two.
29. The best theater tickets cost from three to six dollars.
30. Thursday and Sunday were hot, but today is nice.

H. Sentences with / d /, / ð /, and / z /
31. Their ideas are always good.
32. They have Wednesday off, don't they?
33. These old roads are in bad condition.
34. Is his father a doctor?

GROUP X | Consonants / f, v, w, h, y, j, č, š /

PRONUNCIATION DRILL 21

1. CONSONANTS / f, v, w /

Words Frequently Used

In English, the "ƒ sound" is made by touching the upper teeth to the lower lip, and letting the breath come out between them. The sounds /f/ and /v/ are alike, except that the "ƒ sound" is voiceless, like /t/.

Practice the following common words containing the "ƒ sound" /f/, as in *fine*.

fine	four	coffee	life
for	five	different	off
first	fourteen	awful	if
find	fifteen	information	laugh
family	forty	telephone	leaf

Sentences

1. They went to the cafeteria for some coffee.
2. California has a fine climate.
3. This room has comfortable furniture.
4. If you don't know the telephone number, call information.

2.   THE CONSONANT / v /

Words Frequently Used

The "*v* sound" is made by the upper teeth touching the lower lip.

Practice the following common words containing the "*v* sound" /v/, as in *very*.

very	visit	November	live
V	vegetable	of	five
verb	seven	over	move
vowel	eleven	ever	have
vacant	seventeen	every	leave
vacation	seventy	never	believe
value	evening	several	twelve

Sentences

5. I live very near Avery Avenue.
6. All English vowels are voiced.
7. Have you ever visited Vicksburg?
8. Five and seven make twelve.   (5+7=12)

3.   CONSONANTS / f, v /

Words in Contrast

Now you will hear some pairs of words which differ only in having the "*f* sound" /f/, as in *fine*, or the "*v* sound" /v/, as in *vine*. Remember that the position of the lips and teeth is the same for these two sounds. The only difference is that /f/ is voiceless, like /t/, and /v/ is voiced, like /d/. In the pairs below, the first word has /f/, and the second word has /v/.

fine, vine	life, live	leaf, leave	fan, van
belief, believe	file, vile	fee, V	few, view
feel, veal	fat, vat	half, halve	shuffle, shovel
raffle, ravel	feign, vane	fear, veer	foil, voile

Sentences

9. During the first fall days, the leaves turn lovely colors.
10. Do you find the English verbs very difficult?
11. I believe President Roosevelt died in 1945.
12. I'd like to move to the boarding house if there's a comfortable room vacant.

4. THE CONSONANT / w /

Words Frequently Used

The "*w* sound" in English is made with the lips rounded, and the tongue high and back at the beginning of the sound. The sound is voiced, like /d/.

Practice the following common words containing the "*w* sound" /w/, as in *week*.

week	wait	won't	were
one	work	wonder	was
well	wish	welcome	willing
woman	will	window	weather
women	with	anyway	weight
want	would	warm	world

NOTE: Several common English words spelled with *wh* are pronounced by some Americans with the /hw/ sound, and by others with the /w/ sound. Either is correct. Imitate your teacher and the other educated speakers around you. The most common words in this category are *where, why, when, what,* and *which.*

Sentences

13. We always walk to work.
14. One day a week, we usually wash our clothes.
15. Why do you want to know?
16. The weather was warm this week, wasn't it?

5. CONSONANTS / w, v /

Words in Contrast

Now you will hear some pairs of words which differ in having the "*w* sound" /w/, as in *wine*, or the "*v* sound" /v/, as in *vine*. The first word has /w/; the second word has /v/.

wet, vet	wow, vow	we, V	wine, vine
wane, vane	wiper, viper	Willa, villa	wail, veil
went, vent	west, vest	wick, Vic	

Sentences

17. Why can't Washingtonians ever vote?
18. When our friends leave, we wave good-bye to them.
19. Are Nevada and Wyoming western states?
20. I believe Virginia and West Virginia are very near Washington.

6. CONSONANTS / f, v, w /

Review Sentences

Review the sentences you practiced in PD 21.

A. Sentences with / f /
   1. They went to the cafeteria for some coffee.
   2. California has a fine climate.
   3. This room has comfortable furniture.
   4. If you don't know the telephone number, call information.

B. Sentences with / v /

    5. I live very near Avery Avenue.
    6. All English vowels are voiced.
    7. Have you ever visited Vicksburg?
    8. Five and seven make twelve. (5+7=12)

C. Sentences with / f / and / v /

    9. During the first fall days, the leaves turn lovely colors.
  10. Do you find the English verbs very difficult?
  11. I believe President Roosevelt died in 1945.
  12. I'd like to move to the boarding house if there's a comfortable room vacant.

D. Sentences with / w /

  13. We always walk to work.
  14. One day a week, we usually wash our clothes.
  15. Why do you want to know?
  16. The weather was warm this week, wasn't it?

E. Sentences with / w / and / v /

  17. Why can't Washingtonians ever vote?
  18. When our friends leave, we wave good-bye to them.
  19. Are Nevada and Wyoming western states?
  20. I believe Virginia and West Virginia are very near Washington.

PRONUNCIATION DRILL 22

7. THE CONSONANT / h /

Words Frequently Used

The "h sound" in English is made by blowing the breath out. The lips and tongue are in the position for the following sound.

Practice the following common words containing the "h sound" /h/, as in *here*.

here	hundred	house	hand
hear	home	head	habit
how	ahead	heavy	half
hello	help	heard	hair
high	hard	hot	heat
who	hope	horse	health
whose	hotel	heart	human

Sentences

1. Here's your hat.
2. He likes hot dogs and hamburgers.
3. Is that a boarding house or a hotel?
4. How hot it is in here!

8. THE CONSONANT / h /

Words in Contrast

Now you will hear some pairs of words which differ in having or not having the "*h* sound" /h/, as in *here*. The first word does not have /h/; the second word has /h/.

ill, hill	am, ham	all, hall	air, hair
eat, heat	it, hit	at, hat	E, he
ear, hear	is, his	eye, hi	as, has
add, had	Ed, head	art, heart	and, hand
A, hay	ate, hate	odd, hod	old, hold
all, hall	owl, howl	arm, harm	ale, hale

Sentences

5. Is it *his* hat?
6. We hear with our ears.
7. Hello, Ellen.
8. I hate ham, but I ate it anyway.

9. THE CONSONANT / y /

Words Frequently Used

At the beginning of the "*y* sound" the tongue is in a high position toward the front of the mouth. The middle of the tongue is near the hard palate. The tip of the tongue does *not* touch the ridge just behind the teeth.

Practice the following common words containing the "*y* sound" /y/, as in *you*.

you	year	yes	billion
your	usually	yesterday	young
January	use (v.)	yet	beyond
excuse	use (n.)	yellow	yard
United States	few	million	Yankee

Sentences

9. Do you practice your English in class?
10. Is your sister younger than you?
11. Yale is a famous university in the United States.
12. Last year, they used to play tennis every day.

10. THE CONSONANT / j /

Words Frequently Used

During the first part of the "*j* sound," the tip of the tongue touches the ridge just behind the upper teeth. The lips are pushed out a little. The "*j* sound" is voiced, like /d/.

Practice the following common words containing the "*j* sound" /j/, as in *job*.

job	joke	vegetable	large
G, J	Jack	subject	marriage
January	James	religion	George
June	jazz	engine	judge
July	germ	soldier	package
just	general	Georgia	language

Sentences

13. June, July, and January begin with *j*.
14. We have orange juice, grapefruit juice, and pineapple juice.
15. Did Jack and Joe just come?
16. George got a job selling vegetables.

11. CONSONANTS / y, j /

Words in Contrast

Now you will hear some pairs of words which differ in having the "*y* sound" /y/, as in *yet*, or the "*j* sound" /j/, as in *jet*. The first word has /y/; the second word has /j/.

yam, jam	yet, jet	use, juice	yellow, jello
yell, jell	yoke, joke	yak, Jack	you, Jew
year, jeer	Yale, jail	yard, jarred	yacht, jot
ye, G	use, Jews	yea, Jay	yon, John

Sentences

17. Lemon jello is yellow.
18. Have you flown in a jet plane yet?
19. Jack and George go to Yale University.
20. I like yams with ham, but not jam with ham.

12. CONSONANTS / h, y, j /

Review Sentences

Review the sentences you practiced in PD 22.

A. Sentences with / h /
1. Here's your hat.
2. He likes hot dogs and hamburgers.
3. Is that a boarding house or a hotel?
4. How hot it is in here!

B. Sentences with / h / in contrast with initial vowel sound

    5. Is it *his* hat?
    6. We hear with our ears.
    7. Hello, Ellen.
    8. I hate ham, but I ate it anyway.

C. Sentences with / y /

    9. Do you practice your English in class?
  10. Is your sister younger than you?
  11. Yale is a famous university in the United States.
  12. Last year, they used to play tennis every day.

D. Sentences with / j /

  13. June, July, and January begin with *j*.
  14. We have orange juice, grapefruit juice, and pineapple juice.
  15. Did Jack and Joe just come?
  16. George got a job selling vegetables.

E. Sentences with / y / and / j /

  17. Lemon jello is yellow.
  18. Have you flown in a jet plane yet?
  19. Jack and George go to Yale University.
  20. I like yams with ham, but not jam with ham.

PRONUNCIATION DRILL 23

13. CONSONANTS / č, š, j /

Words Frequently Used

The "*ch* sound" in English is made with the tongue close to the palate, and the lips pushed out a little. The tip of the tongue touches the ridge just behind the upper teeth during the first part of the sound. The /č/ is voiceless like /t/, but otherwise it is like /j/.

Practice the following common words containing the "*ch* sound" /č/, as in *child*.

child	check	teacher	much
children	chair	lecture	watch
chicken	cheap	furniture	teach
cheese	chin	actual	such
change	choose	luncheon	H

Sentences

1. The child was born in March.
2. Do you want a cheese sandwich or a chicken sandwich?
3. Which lecture did the teacher go to?
4. Don't choose a cheap watch.

14. THE CONSONANT / š /

Words Frequently Used

The "*sh* sound" in English is made with the tip of the tongue close to the ridge behind the upper teeth, but *not* touching it. The tongue is curved; that is, the sides are higher than the middle. The lips are pushed out a little. The /š/ is voiceless, like /t/.

Practice the following common words containing the "*sh* sound" /š/, as in *she*.

she	short	direction	wish
shall	show	instructions	wash
should	shouldn't	special	cash
shoe	Chicago	examination	cashier
sure	shower	nation	shave
sugar	shop	national	shine

Sentences

5. She has some new dishes.
6. The instructions should show you how to use the machine.
7. Shall we wash our clothes or brush them?
8. I wish my shoes were shined!

15. CONSONANTS / č, š /

Words in Contrast

Now you will hear some pairs of words which differ in having the "*sh* sound" /š/, as in *ship*, or the "*ch* sound" /č/ as in *chip*. The first word has /š/; the second word has /č/.

ship, chip	shoe, chew	mush, much	marsh, march
dish, ditch	shop, chop	sheep, cheap	shoes, choose
wish, witch	cash, catch	washing, watching	mash, match
share, chair	she's, cheese	shin, chin	

Sentences

9. Are you sure she has two children?
10. Where can I cash a check?
11. He's going to shave and take a shower before lunch.
12. We're watching conditions in Washington.

16. CONSONANTS / č, j /

Words in Contrast

Remember that the /č/ and /j/ are alike, except that /č/ is voiceless like /t/, and /j/ is voiced like /d/.

Now you will hear some pairs of words which differ in having the "*ch* sound" /č/, as in *chin,* or the "*j* sound" /j/, as in *gin*.

chin, gin	cheep, jeep	etching, edging
larch, large	chew, Jew	chest, jest
match, Madge	Chet, jet	batch, badge
		choke, joke

Sentences

13. The children had vegetables and fruit juice for lunch.
14. George bought that chair last July.

15. Which subject does Mr. Jackson teach?
16. Did Charles and Joe enjoy the lecture?

17.   CONSONANTS / č, š, j /

Review Sentences

Review the sentences you practiced in PD 23.

A. Sentences with / č /

1. The child was born in March.
2. Do you want a cheese sandwich or a chicken sandwich?
3. Which lecture did the teacher go to?
4. Don't choose a cheap watch.

B. Sentences with / š /

5. She has some new dishes.
6. The instructions should show you how to use the machine.
7. Shall we wash our clothes or brush them?
8. I wish my shoes were shined!

C. Sentences with / š / or / č /

9. Are you sure she has two children?
10. Where can I cash a check?
11. He's going to shave and take a shower before lunch.
12. We're watching conditions in Washington.

D. Sentences with / č / and / j /

13. The children had vegetables and fruit juice for lunch.
14. George bought that chair last July.
15. Which subject does Mr. Jackson teach?
16. Did Charles and Joe enjoy the lecture?

GROUP XI | **Single Consonants**

PRONUNCIATION DRILL 24

1. CONSONANTS / p, b, v /

Words Frequently Used

In English, the "*p* sound" and the "*b* sound" are both made by closing the lips and then opening them. The "*p* sound" is voiceless, like /t/, and the "*b* sound" is voiced, like /d/.

Practice the following common words containing the "*p* sound" /p/, as in *person*.

person	piece	people	keep
put	pie	couple	hope
P	pound	happen	up
pay	pack	simple	cup
possibly	suppose	open	map

Sentences

1. Please pay the cashier.
2. I'd like a piece of apple pie and a cup of coffee, please.
3. Paul, did you put the paper on the desk?
4. Don't push other people.

2. CONSONANT / b /

Words Frequently Used

Practice the following common words containing the "*b* sound" /b/, as in *be*.

be	Bob	bus	November
B	job	busy	December
big	baby	billion	cab
Boston	back	bad	best
about	but	good-bye	believe
possible	by	October	probably

Sentences

5. "Better" and "best" begin with B.
6. Bob's from Boston, I believe.
7. Will you be back by October?
8. Isn't this new building beautiful?

3. CONSONANTS / p, b /

Words in Contrast

Now you will hear some pairs of words which differ in having the "*p* sound" /p/, as in *pea*, or the "*b* sound" /b/, as in *be*. The first word has /p/; the second word has /b/.

pay, bay	pin, bin	maple, Mabel	sopping, sobbing
nip, nib	mop, mob	napped, nabbed	putt, but
pie, by	pound, bound	pack, back	cup, cub
Pete, beet	pet, bet		

Sentences

9. The program will probably begin about eight o'clock.
10. Pears and bananas are both fruits, but potatoes are vegetables.
11. Paul, you'd better buy this paper.
12. Which bus goes to the Capitol?

4. CONSONANTS / b, v /

Words in Contrast

Remember that the "*b* sound" is made by closing the lips and then opening them, and that the "*v* sound" is made by the upper teeth touching the lower lip.

Now you will hear some pairs of words which differ in having the "*b* sound" /b/, as in *bat*, or the "*v* sound" /v/, as in *vat*. The first word has /b/; the second word has /v/.

bat, vat	Boyd, void	by, vie	bet, vet
Lib, live	bane, vane	boat, vote	bale, veil
boil, voile	bend, vend	saber, saver	robe, rove
cabs, calves	lobes, loaves	berry, very	

Sentences

13. Bill is very much better today.
14. Every boy in school plays volley ball.
15. Do these berries grow on vines or bushes?
16. In English, *B* and *V* are both voiced.

5. CONSONANTS / p, b, v /

Review Sentences

Review the sentences you practiced in PD 24.

A. Sentences with / p /

    1. Please pay the cashier.
    2. I'd like a piece of apple pie and a cup of coffee, please.
    3. Paul, did you put the paper on the desk?
    4. Don't push other people.

B. Sentences with / b /

    5. "Better" and "best" begin with B.
    6. Bob's from Boston, I believe.
    7. Will you be back by October?
    8. Isn't this new building beautiful?

C. Sentences with / p / and / b /

   9. The program will probably begin about eight o'clock.
  10. Pears and bananas are both fruits, but potatoes are vegetables.
  11. Paul, you'd better buy this paper.
  12. Which bus goes to the Capitol?

D. Sentences with / b / and / v /

  13. Bill is very much better today.
  14. Every boy in school plays volley ball.
  15. Do these berries grow on vines or bushes?
  16. In English, *B* and *V* are both voiced.

PRONUNCIATION DRILL 25

6. CONSONANTS / k, g, p, t, č, b, d, j /

Words Frequently Used

In English, the "*k* sound" and the "*g* sound" are made by touching the back part of the tongue to the soft palate. The "*k* sound" is voiceless, like /t/, and the "*g* sound" is voiced, like /d/.

Practice the following common words containing the "*k* sound" /k/, as in *come*.

come	back	car	check
welcome	key	coffee	breakfast
talk	instruction	look	came
call	American	book	cat
take	buckle	like	cake
make	luck	can	steak

Sentences

1. Most Americans have coffee for breakfast.
2. Where can I cash a check?
3. Call me at six o'clock.
4. Is he looking for work in a factory?

7. THE CONSONANT / g /

Words Frequently Used

Practice the following common words containing the "*g* sound" /g/, as in *get*.

get	forget	girl	sugar
give	again	go	cigarette
guess	begin	garden	magazine
game	egg	good	dog
guest	big	August	dialogue

Sentences

5. The girl got eggs, cigarettes, and sugar.
6. Don't forget to study the dialogue.
7. Are you going to begin your vacation in August?
8. Is the weather good for your garden?

8. CONSONANTS / k, g /

Words in Contrast

Now you will hear some pairs of words which differ in having the "*k* sound" /k/, as in *come*, or the "*g* sound" /g/, as in *gum*. The first word has /k/; the second word has /g/.

come, gum	Kay, gay	pick, pig	muck, mug
cull, gull	Kate, gate	plucked, plugged	bicker, bigger
call, gall	could, good	curl, girl	duck, dug
cane, gain	luck, lug	lacking, lagging	leak, league

Sentences

9. He always gets eggs and coffee for breakfast.
10. Call me again some time.
11. Did they get Lucky Strike cigarettes?
12. I've got to go to the bank to cash a check.

9. CONSONANTS / p, t, č, k /

Words Frequently Used

Practice the following common words containing the "*p* sound" /p/, as in *possible*; the "*ch* sound" /č/, as in *child*; the "*t* sound" /t/, as in *time*; or the "*k* sound" /k/, as in *car*.

possible	time	child	car
put	table	cheese	call
open	little	teacher	because
happy	button	lecture	talking
cup	let	much	take
map	not	watch	mark

Sentences

13. I'd like a cup of coffee and a piece of apple pie.
14. Can you tell me the time?
15. Which lecture did the teacher go to?
16. Where can I cash a check?

10. CONSONANTS / b, d, j, g /

Words Frequently Used

Practice the following common words containing the "*b* sound" /b/, as in *big*; the "*d* sound" /d/, as in *do*; the "*j* sound" /j/, as in *June*; and the "*g* sound" /g/, as in *get*.

big	do	June	get
believe	day	job	give
about	ready	vegetable	ago
table	reading	subject	together
job	good	large	bag
cab	bad	marriage	leg

Sentences

17. Bob's from Boston, I believe.

98

18. Ted had a good idea, didn't he?
19. George got a job selling vegetables.
20. Are you going to begin your vacation in August?

11. CONSONANTS / k, g, p, t, č, b, d, j /

Review Sentences

Review the sentences you practiced in PD 25.

A. Sentences with / k /

    1. Most Americans have coffee for breakfast.
    2. Where can I cash a check?
    3. Call me at six o'clock.
    4. Is he looking for work in a factory?

B. Sentences with / g /

    5. The girl got eggs, cigarettes, and sugar.
    6. Don't forget to study the dialogue.
    7. Are you going to begin your vacation in August?
    8. Is the weather good for your garden?

C. Sentences with / k / and / g /

    9. He always gets eggs and coffee for breakfast.
  10. Call me again some time.
  11. Did they get Lucky Strike cigarettes?
  12. I've got to go to the bank to cash a check.

D. Sentences with / p /, / t /, / č /, or / k /

  13. I'd like a cup of coffee and a piece of apple pie.
  14. Can you tell me the time?
  15. Which lecture did the teacher go to?
  16. Where can I cash a check?

E. Sentences with / b /, / d /, / j /, or / g /

  17. Bob's from Boston, I believe.
  18. Ted had a good idea, didn't he?
  19. George got a job selling vegetables.
  20. Are you going to begin your vacation in August?

PRONUNCIATION DRILL 26

12. THE CONSONANT / ž /

Words Frequently Used

The "*zh* sound" in English is made with the tip of the tongue close to the ridge just behind the upper teeth, but not touching it. The tongue is curved; that is, the sides are higher than the middle. The lips are often pushed out a little. The "*zh* sound" is voiced, like /d/. This sound occurs in the middle and at the end of English words, but not at the beginning.

Practice the following common words containing the "*zh* sound" /ž/, as in *measure*.

measure	division	collision	garage[1]
vision	confusion	decision	beige[1]
pleasure	conclusion	leisure	rouge[1]

Sentences

1. I have to measure the garage.
2. The collision occurred because of the driver's poor vision.

13. CONSONANTS / š, ž /

Words in Contrast

Now you will hear some pairs of words which differ in having the "*sh* sound" /š/, as in *Aleutian*, or the "*zh* sound" /ž/, as in *allusion*. Remember that the mouth position is the same for these sounds, but /š/ is voiceless, like /t/, and /ž/ is voiced, like /d/.

ruche, rouge	Asher, azure
Aleutian, allusion	dilution, delusion
mesher, measure	fission, vision
glacier, glazier	Confucian, confusion

---

[1]Some speakers pronounce these words with /j/, not /ž/.

Sentences

3. It's a pleasure to see you, Mr. Shaw.
4. Could you give me directions to the Treasury Building?
5. After making an examination, the doctor will give his decision.
6. She wore a beige suit and red shoes.

14. CONSONANTS / f, θ, s, š /

Words Frequently Used

Practice the following common words with the "*f* sound" /f/, as in *face*; the voiceless "*th* sound" /θ/, as in *thank*; the "*s* sound" /s/, as in *see*; and the "*sh* sound" /š/, as in *she*.

face	thank	see	she
five	thought	say	sure
office	nothing	possibly	special
before	mathematical	listen	direction
if	breath	nice	cash
life	south	place	wish

Sentences

7. They went to the cafeteria for some coffee.
8. I thought I'd go south, not north.
9. Did your sister send this to us?
10. Shall we wash our clothes or brush them?

15. CONSONANTS / v, ð, z, ž /

Words Frequently Used

Practice the following common words containing the "*v* sound" /v/, as in *very*; the voiced "*th* sound" /ð/, as in *this*; the "*z* sound" /z/, as in *zoo*; or the "*zh* sound" /ž/, as in *measure*.

very	this	zoo	measure
visit	that	zero	vision

every	another	thousand	confusion
ever	rather	Tuesday	division
five	smooth	was	garage
have	bathe	always	rouge

Sentences

11. I live very near Avery Avenue.
12. My brothers did that themselves.
13. He always goes to the zoo on Thursdays.
14. I have to measure the garage.

16. CONSONANTS / f, v, s, z, θ, ð, š, ž/

Review Sentences

Review the sentences you practiced in PD 26.

A. Sentences with / ž /

1. I have to measure the garage.
2. The collision occurred because of the driver's poor vision.

B. Sentences with / š / and / ž /

3. It's a pleasure to see you, Mr. Shaw.
4. Could you give me directions to the Treasury Building?
5. After making an examination, the doctor will give his decision.
6. She wore a beige suit and red shoes.

C. Sentences with / f /, / θ /, / s /, and / š /

7. They went to the cafeteria for some coffee.
8. I thought I'd go south, not north.
9. Did your sister send this to us?
10. Shall we wash our clothes or brush them?

D. Sentences with / v /, / ð /, / z /, and / ž /

11. I live very near Avery Avenue.
12. My brothers did that themselves.
13. He always goes to the zoo on Thursdays.
14. I have to measure the garage.

PRONUNCIATION DRILL 27

17. CONSONANTS / r, l /

Words Frequently Used

The "*r* sound" in English may be made in several different ways. The "*r* sound" before a vowel may be made by turning the tip of the tongue up toward the palate. The tongue does not touch the palate, and it does not vibrate. The /r/ is voiced, like /d/.

The "*l* sound" before vowels, as in *leap*, is made with the front of the tongue touching the ridge just behind the teeth, and the middle of the tongue high. The "*l* sound" after vowels, as in *call*, is made with the tip of the tongue touching the ridge behind the teeth, and with the back of the tongue high. Some speakers have only one variety of *l*, the "back *l*," as in *call*, which they use everywhere.

Practice the following common words containing the "*r* sound" before vowels, /r/, as in *right*.

right	run	ready	wrap
read	real	red	restaurant
ring	rice	rock	rich
railroad	radio	wrote	really
room	rain	remind	rates

Sentences

1. It's raining rather hard today.
2. Are you ready to go, Robert?
3. Rachel's roommate is named Ruth.
4. Would you rather have a radio or a record player?

18. THE CONSONANT / l /

Words Frequently Used

Practice the following common words containing the "*l* sound" /l/, as in *let* and *call*.

let	look	eleven	well
like	low	million	all
last	lie	billion	feel
letter	law	hello	sell
late	lose	July	call

Sentences

5. We all like to get letters.
6. Carolyn lives on Lowell Lane.
7. Do you feel well today?
8. Does he like to look at television?

19.   CONSONANTS / l, r /

Words in Contrast

Now you will hear some pairs of words which differ in having the "*l* sound" /l/, as in *lie*, or the "*r* sound" /r/, as in *rye*. The first word has /l/; the second word has /r/.

lie, rye	line, Rhine	pole, pour	mull, myrrh
dill, deer	look, rook	low, row	lake, rake
list, wrist	light, right	lock, rock	lid, rid
loss, Ross	lace, race	lobe, robe	boll, bore
nil, near		sill, sear	

Sentences

9. Louise writes long letters to her father every Saturday.
10. We had a very long trip to Lexington because we took the wrong road.
11. Does the bell ring regularly at four o'clock?
12. Robert Lane lives in a double room.

104

20. CONSONANTS / l, r /

Words in Contrast

Now you will hear some other pairs of words which differ in having the
"*l* sound" /l/, as in *lie*, or the "*r* sound" /r/, as in *rye*. Here the first word
has /r/, and the second word has /l/.

rid, lid	raid, laid	royal, loyal	reach, leech
ruse, lose	rip, lip	wrap, lap	rot, lot
road, load	rest, lest	root², loot	rag, lag
rear, rill	gore, goal	mire, mile	tore, tall
room, loom	rain, lane		

Sentences

13. I like rare steak.
14. Rose didn't feel well yesterday.
15. Are you looking for a restaurant?
16. Remember to read Lesson Eleven.

21. CONSONANTS / l, r /

Review Sentences

Review the sentences you practiced in PD 27.

A. Sentences with / r /

1. It's raining rather hard today.
2. Are you ready to go, Robert?
3. Rachel's roommate is named Ruth.
4. Would you rather have a radio or a record player?

B. Sentences with / l /

5. We all like to get letters.
6. Carolyn lives on Lowell Lane.
7. Do you feel well today?
8. Does he like to look at television?

---

²Some speakers pronounce this word with /u/, not /uw/.

C. Sentences with / l / and / r /

9. Louise writes long letters to her father every Saturday.
10. We had a very long trip to Lexington because we took the wrong road.
11. Does the bell ring regularly at four o'clock?
12. Robert Lane lives in a double room.
13. I like rare steak.
14. Rose didn't feel well yesterday.
15. Are you looking for a restaurant?
16. Remember to read Lesson Eleven.

PRONUNCIATION DRILL 28

22. CONSONANTS / m, n, ŋ /

Words Frequently Used

The "*m, n,* and *ng* sounds" are nasals. That is, in making these sounds, the mouth passage is closed at some point, and the nose passage is open. All these sounds are voiced, like /d/. The "*m* sound" is made by closing the lips and then opening them. The "*n* sound" is made by touching the tip of the tongue to the ridge just behind the upper teeth. The "*ng* sound" is made by touching the back of the tongue to the velum, or soft palate, behind the roof of the mouth.

Practice the following common words containing the "*m* sound" /m/, as in *much*.

much	Miss	summer	same
many	Mrs.	coming	some
maybe	Mr.	September	come
man	might	November	seem
morning	minute	December	time

Sentences

1. My mother goes to Maine every summer.
2. Maybe Mr. Manning lives on Maple Street.
3. How many women make this much money?
4. What time is it, Miss Hamilton?

23. THE CONSONANT /n/

Words Frequently Used

Practice the following common words containing the "*n* sound" /n/, as in *need*.

need	seven	not	ten
nice	men	Sunday	fourteen
afternoon	women	Monday	in
evening	know	running	can
one	new	nine	then

Sentences

5. I need a new pen.
6. Do you know her name?
7. On Sunday evening, there's a concert at the National Gallery.
8. When can Mr. Nelson come?

24. CONSONANTS / ŋ, ŋg, ŋk /

Words Frequently Used

The letters *ng* are pronounced /ŋ/, as in *long* and *singer*, and they are pronounced /ŋg/, as in *finger* and *longer*. The letters *ng* are also pronounced /nj/, as in *stranger* and *ginger*. Notice that -*ng* is pronounced /ŋ/ at the end of a noun *(thing)* or a verb *(sing)* or a word derived from such a word *(singer)*; it is also pronounced /ŋ/ at the end of adjectives *(long)*.

-*ng* is pronounced /ŋg/ in words like *longer, longest, stronger,* and *strongest,* and in words ending in -*ngle,* etc.—*single, bangle.*

-*nge* is pronounced /nj/ at the end of words—*strange*—and in words derived from such words—*stranger.*

In English, the /ŋ/ never occurs at the beginning of words, and in standard English, /ŋg/ never occurs at the end of words.

Practice the following common words containing the "*ng* sound" /ŋ/, as in *thing*; the "*ngg* sound" /ŋg/, as in *younger*; and the "*nk* sound" /ŋk/, as in *bank.*

/ŋ/	/ŋ/	/ŋg/	/ŋk/
thing	bringing	younger	bank
young	singing	longer	think
song	ringing	single	pink
wrong	hanging	finger	thanking
sing	swinging	stronger	drinking

Sentences

9. How long can you sing without getting tired?
10. Bill Browning always brings the morning paper.
11. This thing is stronger, and it will last longer.
12. I'm thinking of bringing my check to the bank.

25. CONSONANTS, / m, n, ŋ, ŋg, ŋk /

Words in Contrast

Now you will hear some pairs or groups of words which differ in their nasal sound. Each word has one of the following: the "*m* sound" /m/, as in *ram*; the "*n* sound" /n/, as in *ran*; the "*ng* sound" /ŋ/, as in *rang*; the "*ngg* sound" /ŋg/, as in *wrangle*; or the "*nk* sound" /ŋk/, as in *rankle*.

mice, nice	dime, dine
sin, sing	thin, thing
rang, ran, ram	sinner, singer
hang, hangar, anger	tan, tang, tank
ban, bang, bank	
kin, king	Kim, kin, king
rum, rung	rum, run, rung
singer, finger	lawn, long, longer
hung, hunger	bang, banging, bangle
thin, thing, think	

Sentences

13. Mr. Emerson sings tenor.
14. I'm drinking ginger ale, not orange juice.
15. *Kim* is the name of a novel by Kipling.

16. Is John going to New York next Sunday?

26. CONSONANTS / mp, nt, nd, nč /

Words Frequently Used

Practice the following common words containing the "*mp* sounds" /mp/, as in *lamp*; the "*nt* sounds" /nt/, as in *sent*; the "*nd* sounds, /nd/, as in *send*; and the "*nch* sounds" /nč/, as in *lunch*.

lamp	sent	send	lunch
sample	rent	rained	inch
damp	can't	spend	bench
campus	hunt	planned	branch

Sentences

17. This campus is damp in winter.
18. Many students rent rooms near DuPont Circle.
19. We planned to spend the day at the beach, but it rained.
20. He went to an empty bench.

27. CONSONANTS / mp, mb, nd, nt, ŋ, ŋg, ŋk /

Words in Contrast

Now you will hear some pairs and groups of words which differ in having the "*mp* sounds" /mp/, as in *simple*; the "*mb* sounds" /mb/, as in *symbol*; the "*nd* sounds" /nd/, as in *send*; the "*nt* sounds" /nt/, as in *sent*; the "*ng* sounds" /ŋ/, as in *thing*; the "*ngg* sounds" /ŋg/, as in *finger*; or the "*ngk* sounds" /ŋk/, as in *think*.

simple, symbol	ramp, ramble
sent, send	pained, paint
can't, canned	hang, angle, ankle
rang, wrangle, rankle	sing, single, sink
ample, amble	bend, bent
lent, lend	faint, feigned
mound, mount	

Sentences

21. The children in camp rambled through the woods.
22. That letter can't be sent until it's signed.
23. On her way to the bank, Mrs. Young hurt her ankle.
24. The tree bent in the wind.

28. CONSONANTS / m, n, ŋ, mp, nt, nd, nč, mb, ŋg, ŋk /

Review Sentences

Review the sentences you practiced in PD 28.

A. Sentences with / m /

   1. My mother goes to Maine every summer.
   2. Maybe Mr. Manning lives on Maple Street.
   3. How many women make this much money?
   4. What time is it, Miss Hamilton?

B. Sentences with / n /

   5. I need a new pen.
   6. Do you know her name?
   7. On Sunday evening, there's a concert at the National Gallery.
   8. When can Mr. Nelson come?

C. Sentences with / ŋ, ŋg, ŋk /

   9. How long can you sing without getting tired?
  10. Bill Browning always brings the morning paper.
  11. This thing is stronger, and it will last longer.
  12. I'm thinking of bringing my check to the bank.

D. Sentences with / m, n, ŋ, ŋg, ŋk /

  13. Mr. Emerson sings tenor.
  14. I'm drinking ginger ale, not orange juice.
  15. *Kim* is the name of a novel by Kipling.
  16. Is John going to New York next Sunday?

E. Sentences with / mp, nt, nd, nč /

  17. This campus is damp in winter.

110

18. Many students rent rooms near DuPont Circle.
19. We planned to spend the day at the beach, but it rained.
20. He went to an empty bench.

F. Sentences with / mp, mb, nt, nd, ŋ, ŋk /
    21. The children in camp rambled through the woods.
    22. That letter can't be sent until it's signed.
    23. On her way to the bank, Mrs. Young hurt her ankle.
    24. The tree bent in the wind.

GROUP XII | Clusters of / s / + Consonant

PRONUNCIATION DRILL 29

1. / s / CLUSTERS

Words Frequently Used

Remember that /s/ is voiceless. Be careful not to make it voiced when it is followed by a voiced consonant.

Practice the following common words containing the "*sl* sounds" /sl/, as in *slow*, and the "*sw* sounds" /sw/, as in *sweet*.

slow	slot	sweet	swell
sleep	slang	swallow	swing
slip	slippery	swim	Sweden
slice	Slavic	swear	sweetheart

Sentences

1. Swim to shore slowly.
2. Miss Sweeney is sleeping.

2. CONSONANTS / st, sts /

Words Frequently Used

Practice the following common words containing the "*st* sounds" /st/, as in *steak*, and the "*sts* sounds" /sts/, as in *lasts*.

steak	Mister (Mr.)	last	lasts
student	sister	lost	rests
star	yesterday	least	tastes
stand	western	rest	tests

Sentences

3. My sister is a student at Western Reserve University.
4. Mr. Steel always rests after running fast.

3. CONSONANTS / sk, sks /

Words Frequently Used

Practice the following common words containing the "*sk* sounds" /sk/, as in *skin*, and the "*sks* sounds" /sks/, as in *desks*.

skin	scold	escape	desks
sky	skate	ask	risks
school	skip	desk	asks

Sentences

5. There are ten desks in the school room.
6. Ask Mr. Skinner if we can skate here.

4. CONSONANTS / sp, sps /

Words Frequently Used

Practice the following common words containing the "*sp* sounds" /sp/, as in *speak*, and the "*sps* sounds" /sps/, as in *gasps*.

speak	speed	especially	gasps
space	spend	expensive	grasps
special	spelling	hospital	wasps

Sentences

7. We don't eat spinach with a spoon.
8. This hospital is especially good.

5. CONSONANTS / skr, str /

Words Frequently Used

Practice the following common words containing the "*skr* sounds" /skr/, as in *scream*, and the "*str* sounds" /str/, as in *street*.

scream	scrub	street	stranger
scrambled	Scranton	string	strong
scratch	describe	stress	destroy
screen	description	straight	instructions

Sentences

9. I want scrambled eggs, please.
10. All the streets in this town are straight.

6. CONSONANTS / spr, spl, šr /

Words Frequently Used

Practice the following common words containing the "*spr* sounds" /spr/, as in *spring*; the "*spl* sounds" /spl/, as in *splendid*; and the "*shr* sounds" /šr/, as in *shrub*.

spring	splendid	shrub
sprang	splash	shrimp
bed spread	splinter	shrink
spray	splatter	shrine

Sentences

11. Today is a splendid spring day.
12. Shrimp is my favorite seafood.

7. CONSONANTS / sm, sn /

Words Frequently Used

Practice the following common words containing the "*sm* sounds" /sm/, as in *smoke*, or the "*sn* sounds" /sn/, as in *snow*.

smoke	smell	snow	sniff
Smith	smooth	snake	snip
smile	smart	snap	snack
small	smash	sneezing	snob

Sentences

13. Do you smell smoke, Mr. Snow?
14. The Smiths are in the snack bar.

8. / s / CLUSTERS

Review

Review the sentences you have practiced in PD 29.

A. Sentences with / sl / and / sw /
    1. Swim to shore slowly.
    2. Miss Sweeney is sleeping.

B. Sentences with / st / and / sts /
    3. My sister is a student at Western Reserve University.
    4. Mr. Steel always rests after running fast.

C. Sentences with / sk / and / sks /
    5. There are ten desks in the school room.
    6. Ask Mr. Skinner if we can skate here.

D. Sentences with / sp / and / sps /

    7. We don't eat spinach with a spoon.

    8. This hospital is especially good.

E. Sentences with / skr / and / str /

    9. I want scrambled eggs, please.

  10. All the streets in this town are straight.

F. Sentences with / spr /, / spl /, and / šr /

  11. Today is a splendid spring day.

  12. Shrimp is my favorite seafood.

G. Sentences with / sm / and / sn /

  13. Do you smell smoke, Mr. Snow?

  14. The Smiths are in the snack bar.

GROUP XIII | Clusters of Consonant + / l, r /

PRONUNCIATION DRILL 30

1.   / pl, pr, kl, kr, bl, br /

Words Frequently Used

Practice the following common words containing the "*pl* sounds" /pl/, as in *please*, or the "*pr* sounds" /pr/, as in *probably*.

please	airplane	probably	previous
place	employ	price	April
plan	unpleasant	practice	improve
plenty	apply	professor	approve

Sentences

1. Please find out what time the plane leaves.
2. We'll probably see Professor White in April.

2. CONSONANTS / pl, pr /

Words in Contrast

Now you will hear some pairs of words which differ in having the "*pl* sounds" /pl/, as in *play*, or the "*pr* sounds" /pr/, as in *pray*. The first word has /pl/; the second word has /pr/.

play, pray	plate, prate	applies, apprise
plank, prank	plies, prize	plied, pride
plays, praise	plowed, proud	plow, prow
ply, pry	plod, prod	pleasant, present

Sentences

3. They plan to practice tonight.
4. What's the price of these pretty plates?

3. CONSONANTS / kl, kr /

Words Frequently Used

Practice the following common words containing the "*kl* sounds" /kl/, as in *class*, or the "*kr* sounds" /kr/, as in *cross*.

class	close (v.)	cross	crazy
clean	close (adj.)	cream	across
club	climate	cracker	crowd
closet	clothing	criminal	cry

Sentences

5. In this climate, you need warm clothing.
6. He went across the street to buy some ice cream.

4. CONSONANTS / kl, kr /

Words in Contrast

Now you will hear some pairs of words which differ in having the "*kl* sounds" /kl/, as in *clown*, or the "*kr* sounds" /kr/, as in *crown*. The first word has /kl/; the second word has /kr/.

clown, crown	Clyde, cried	clamp, cramp
clack, crack	clabber, crabber	class, crass
cloak, croak	clash, crash	clue, crew
clank, crank	close, crows	clam, cram
climb, crime	click, crick	

Sentences

7. On a clear day, we can see across the valley.
8. Was the club house crowded last night?

5. CONSONANTS / bl, br /

Words Frequently Used

Practice the following common words containing the "*bl* sounds" /bl/, as in *black*, or the "*br* sounds" /br/, as in *brown*.

black	blood	brown	bread
blue	blind	breakfast	brother
blow	blink	bring	break
blank	blame	brave	breath

Sentences

9. The Blanding School colors are blue and black.
10. Bring my brother's breakfast, please.

6. CONSONANTS / bl, br /

Words in Contrast

Now you will hear some pairs of words which differ in having the "*bl* sounds" /bl/, as in *blue*, or the "*br* sounds" /br/, as in *brew*. The first word has /bl/; the second word has /br/.

blue, brew	blanch, branch	blouse, browse
Blake, break	bleach, breach	bled, bread
blain, brain	bloom, broom	blade, braid
blazon, brazen	bland, brand	blandish, brandish
blight, bright	blackish, brackish	bleed, breed
blink, brink	blush, brush	blues, bruise
blaze, braise	blest, breast	

Sentences

11. My brother bought black shoes and a brown hat.
12. Today the wind is blowing and the sun is shining brightly.

7. CONSONANTS / pl, pr, kl, kr, bl, br /

Review Sentences

Review the sentences you practiced in PD 30.

A. Sentences with / pl / and / pr /

1. Please find out what time the plane leaves.
2. We'll probably see Professor White in April.
3. They plan to practice tonight.
4. What's the price of these pretty plates?

B. Sentences with / kl / and / kr /

5. In this climate, you need warm clothing.
6. He went across the street to buy some ice cream.
7. On a clear day, we can see across the valley.
8. Was the club house crowded last night?

C. Sentences with / bl / and / br /

9. The Blanding School colors are blue and black.
10. Bring my brother's breakfast, please.
11. My brother bought black shoes and a brown hat.
12. Today the wind is blowing and the sun is shining brightly.

PRONUNCIATION DRILL 31

8. CONSONANTS / gl, gr, fl, fr /

Words Frequently Used

Practice the following common words containing the *"gl* sounds" /gl/, as in *glad*, or the *"gr* sounds" /gr/, as in *great*.

glad	glorious	great	grow
glass	globe	green	ground
glove	glue	grass	group

Sentences

1. Was Gloria glad to see you?
2. The grass is very green now.

9. CONSONANTS / gl, gr /

Words in Contrast

Now you will hear some words which differ in having the *"gl* sounds" /gl/, as in *glue*, or the *"gr* sounds" /gr/, as in *grew*. The first word has /gl/; the second word has /gr/.

glass, grass	gland, grand	glaze, graze
glade, grade	glad, grad	glean, green
gloom, groom	glow, grow	glimmer, grimmer
glue, grew		

Sentences

3. I'm glad the grass is growing.
4. That group of students is from Glasgow.

10. CONSONANTS / fl, fr /

Words Frequently Used

Practice the following common words containing the "*fl* sounds" /fl/, as in *flag*, or the "*fr* sounds" /fr/, as in *free*.

flag	float	free	from
flat	floor	France	front
fly	flower	fresh	fruit

Sentences

5. This seaplane flies and also floats on the water.
6. Do you prefer fresh fruit or frozen fruit?

11. CONSONANTS / fl, fr /

Words in Contrast

Now you will hear some pairs of words which differ in having the "*fl* sounds" /fl/, as in *flee*, or the "*fr* sounds" /fr/, as in *free*. The first word has /fl/; the second word has /fr/.

flee, free	flesh, fresh	fly, fry	flute, fruit
flank, frank	flail, frail	flame, frame	flay, fray
fleas, freeze	flier, frier	flight, fright	flow, fro
flock, frock	flog, frog		

Sentences

7. Which flag is flying in front of the embassy?
8. Fred and Florence are from Florida.

12. CONSONANTS / gl, gr, fl, fr /

Review Sentences

Review the sentences you practiced in PD 31.

A. Sentences with / gl / and / gr /

1. Was Gloria glad to see you?
2. The grass is very green now.
3. I'm glad the grass is growing.
4. That group of students is from Glasgow.

B. Sentences with / fl / and / fr /

5. This seaplane flies and also floats on the water.
6. Do you prefer fresh fruit or frozen fruit?
7. Which flag is flying in front of the embassy?
8. Fred and Florence are from Florida.

PRONUNCIATION DRILL 32

13. CONSONANTS / tr, θr, dr /

Words Frequently Used

Practice the following common words with the "*tr* sounds" /tr/, as in *tree*; the "voiceless *th* and *r* sounds" /θ/, as in *three*; and the "*dr* sounds" /dr/, as in *drive*.

tree	three	drive
true	through	drink
try	throw	dress
train	thread	drop

Sentences

1. It's a two-hour trip by train.
2. Did the boys throw the ball through the window?
3. Please drive me to the drugstore.

14. CONSONANTS / tr, θr /

Words in Contrast

Now you will hear some pairs of words which differ in having the "*tr* sounds" /tr/, as in *tree*, or the "voiceless *th* and *r* sounds" /θr/, as in *three*. The first word has /tr/; the second word has /θr/.

tree, three	trash, thrash
trice, thrice	true, threw
trip, thrip	tread, thread
trill, thrill	trust, thrust

Sentences

4. He took a trip through three states.
5. Try to put the thread through the eye of the needle.
6. Mr. Truman's business is thriving.

15. OTHER CONSONANT CLUSTERS

You have now studied the groups of consonants which appear frequently at the beginning and in the middle of words in English.

The following is a review of clusters resulting from "long *u*" after a consonant, C + /yuw/, which you studied in PD 10, Section 5, and of clusters consisting of consonants + /w/.

Say these words with the "long *u*" sound:

/py/	pure, pewter
/ky/	cute, curious
/by/	beauty, beautiful
/gy/	gewgaw, argue
/fy/	few, furious
/vy/	view, revue
/my/	music, mute
/hy/	human, humorous

Now say these combinations with /w/:

/tw/	twin, twenty
/kw/	quiet, quick
/dw/	dwarf, dwell
/gw/	guava, Gwen
/θw/	thwart, thwack
/sw/	swim, swarm
/šw/	Schwartz, Schwinn

126

Now say these words containing groups of consonants with either the "long *u*" or the /w/ sound:

/spy/   spew, dispute
/sky/   skewer, askew
/skw/   squeeze, squabble

Now listen to these sentences containing the sounds you just reviewed.

1. Walt Disney invented a few cute dwarfs.
2. Hugh thought the twins were beautiful.
3. There is no quick cure for that dispute.
4. The minor squabble became a feud.
5. Isn't this a beautiful view?
6. The music here is usually quiet and beautiful.

GROUP XIV | Clusters of / r / + Consonant

PRONUNCIATION DRILL 33

1. CONSONANTS / rp, rt, rč, rk /

Words Frequently Used

The "*r* sound" followed by a consonant occurs in the middle and at the end of English words. If time permits, review Pronunciation Drills 13 and 14, where vowels before *r* are given.

Practice the following common words containing the "*rp* sounds" /rp/, as in *sharp*; the "*rt* sounds" /rt/, as in *heart*; the "*rch* sounds" /rč/, as in *church*; and the "*rk* sounds" /rk/, as in *work*.

sharp	heart	church	work
purple	dirty	search	fork
Antwerp	porch	March	circle
Harper	part	arch	parking

Sentences

1. Please sharpen this purple pencil.
2. Bert spilled dessert on his shirt at the party.
3. Many churches have Gothic arches.
4. Does Mark work in New York?

2. CONSONANTS / rb, rd, rg, rj /

Words Frequently Used

Practice the following common words containing the "*rb* sounds" /rb/, as in *barber*; the "*rd* sounds" /rd/, as in *word*; the "*rg* sounds" /rg/, as in *Pittsburgh*; and the "*rj* sounds" /rj/, as in *urge*.

barber	word	Pittsburgh	urge
harbor	heard	iceberg	large
suburb	third	cargo	charge
absorb	cured	target	sergeant

Sentences

5. Is there a barber shop in this suburb?
6. I heard every word you said.
7. The ship hit an iceberg and the cargo sank.
8. Does the sergeant have a large car?

3. CONSONANTS / rf, rθ, rv, rð /

Words Frequently Used

Practice the following common words containing the "*rf* sounds" /rf/, as in *careful*; the "*r* voiceless *th* sounds" /rθ/, as in *fourth*; the "*rv* sounds" /rv/, as in *curve*; and the "*r* voiced *th* sounds" /rð/, as in *further*.

careful	fourth	curve	further
orphan	earth	serve	farther
scarf	birth	deserve	farthest
perfect	north	nerve	northern

Sentences

9. The scarf matches perfectly.
10. His birthplace was North Carolina.
11. Does it make you nervous when a car goes around a curve too fast?
12. Northern New York is farther from here than you think.

4. CONSONANTS / rs, rš, rz, rž /

Words Frequently Used

Practice the following common words containing the "*rs* sounds" /rs/, as in *person*; the "*rsh* sounds" /rš/, as in *harsh*; the "*rz* sounds" /rz/, as in *stairs*; and the "*rzh* sounds" /rž/, as in *Persia*.

person	harsh	stairs	Persia
worse	marsh	hers	Persian
nurse	partial	Thursday	version
horse	portion	cars	aversion

Sentences

13. A person who writes verse is called a poet.
14. Have you heard of the Marshall Plan?
15. Are these cars *both* hers?
16. Does he speak Persian?

5. CONSONANTS / rl, rm, rn /

Words Frequently Used

Practice the following common words containing the "*rl* sounds" /rl/, as in *girl*; the "*rm* sounds" /rm/, as in *arm*; and the "*rn* sounds" /rn/, as in *learn*.

girl	arm	learn
curl	permanent	turn
early	storm	modern
Arlington	farm	morning

Sentences

17. Does the girl have curly hair?
18. Will they live on the farm permanently?
19. What did you learn this morning?

6. / r / FOLLOWED BY A CONSONANT

Review Sentences

Review the sentences you practiced in PD 33.

A. Sentences with / rp /, / rt /, / rč /, and / rk /

1. Please sharpen this purple pencil.
2. Bert spilled dessert on his shirt at the party.
3. Many churches have Gothic arches.
4. Does Mark work in New York?

B. Sentences with / rb /, / rd /, / rg /, and / rj /

5. Is there a barber shop in this suburb?
6. I heard every word you said.
7. The ship hit an iceberg and the cargo sank.
8. Does the sergeant have a large car?

C. Sentences with / rf /, / rθ /, / rv /, and / rð /

9. The scarf matches perfectly.
10. His birthplace was North Carolina.
11. Does it make you nervous when a car goes around a curve too fast?
12. Northern New York is farther from here than you think.

D. Sentences with / rs /, / rš /, / rz /, and / rž /

13. A person who writes verse is called a poet.
14. Have you heard of the Marshall Plan?
15. Are these cars *both* hers?
16. Does he speak Persian?

E. Sentences with / rl /, / rm /, and / rn /

17. Does the girl have curly hair?
18. Will they live on the farm permanently?
19. What did you learn this morning?

GROUP XV | Final Clusters Ending in / s, z, t, d /

PRONUNCIATION DRILL 34

1. CONSONANTS / ps, ts, fs, θs, pt, kt, ft, st, št, čt /

Words Frequently Used

NOTE: Review PD 15 before doing this lesson.

Below are some nouns ending in /ps/, /ts/, /ks/, /fs/, and /θs/, in their possessive and plural forms, made by adding the "*s* sound" to the singular form of the noun. Practice these words containing final consonant clusters.

caps	minutes	weeks	wife's	berths
maps	streets	thanks	handkerchiefs	Ruth's
cups	coats	backs	laughs	breaths
shops	dates	books	coughs	deaths

Sentences

1. These shops don't sell maps.
2. She's always at least ten minutes late for dates.
3. Thanks for the books.
4. Those are my wife's handkerchiefs.
5. Ruth's job is recording the births and deaths in this city.

133

2. CONSONANTS / ps, ts, ks, fs /

Words Frequently Used

Below are some verbs ending in /ps/, /ts/, /ks/, and /fs/, in the third person singular present tense form, made by adding the "s sound" to the simple form of the verb.[1] Practice these words containing final consonant clusters.

stops	writes	takes	laughs
keeps	sits	checks	coughs
sleeps	lets	makes	stuffs
hopes	gets	talks	telegraphs

Sentences

6. Mr. Brown usually stops work at noon and sleeps for an hour.
7. She sits in the park every day and waits for her friend.
8. He always walks and talks with me.
9. She always laughs at us.

3. CONSONANTS / pt, kt, ft /

Words Frequently Used

Below are some verbs ending in /pt/, /kt/, and /ft/ in their past tense form, made in regular verbs by adding the "t sound" to the simple form of the verb.[2] Remember that although regular verbs add the letters -ed to form the past tense, the pronunciation is /t/ when the verb ends in /p/, /k/, or /f/. Practice the words below ending in final consonant clusters.

stopped	talked	laughed
hoped	liked	coughed
kept	walked	left
slept	looked	telegraphed

---

[1]Verbs ending in /θ/, such as *froth*, also form the third person singular present tense form by adding /s/, but such verbs are rare.

[2]Verbs ending in /θ/, such as *froth*, also form the past tense by adding /t/, but such verbs are rare.

Sentences

10. They stopped in Chicago and slept.
11. We checked our suitcases at the station and walked around the city.
12. I wonder why he laughed when he left.

4. CONSONANTS / st, št, čt /

Words Frequently Used

Below are some verbs ending in /st/, /št/, and /čt/ in their past tense form. Practice these words containing final consonant clusters.

passed	finished	watched
danced	wished	reached
noticed	rushed	touched
missed	cashed	scratched

Sentences

13. They danced until midnight.
14. I finished my homework at nine o'clock.
15. We watched television last night.

5. FINAL CONSONANT CLUSTERS

Review Sentences

Review the sentences you have practiced in PD 34.

A. Sentences with / ps /, / ts /, / ks /, and / θs /
1. These shops don't sell maps.
2. She's always at least ten minutes late for dates.
3. Thanks for the books.
4. Those are my wife's handkerchiefs.
5. Ruth's job is recording the births and deaths in this city.
6. Mr. Brown usually stops work at noon and sleeps for an hour.

7. She sits in the park every day and waits for her friend.
8. He always walks and talks with me.
9. She always laughs at us.

B. Sentences with / pt /, / kt /, and / ft /

10. They stopped in Chicago and slept.
11. We checked our suitcases at the station and walked around the city.
12. I wonder why he laughed when he left.

C. Sentences with / st /, / št /, and / čt /

13. They danced until midnight.
14. I finished my homework at nine o'clock.
15. We watched television last night.

PRONUNCIATION DRILL 35

6. CONSONANTS / bz, dz, gz, vz, ðz /

Words Frequently Used

Below are some nouns ending in /bz/, /dz/, /gz/, /vz/, and /ðz/ in their possessive and plural forms, regularly made by adding the "z sound" to the singular form of the noun. Practice these words containing final consonant clusters.

cabs	Ed's	dogs	wives	paths
clubs	beds	eggs	leaves	baths
jobs	heads	legs	knives	
Bob's	roads	drugs	lives	

Sentences

1. Bob's sister has two jobs.
2. These beds are more comfortable than Ed's.
3. Both the dog's legs are hurt.
4. Mr. Ives and Mr. Cleaves have been friends all their lives.
5. Does the new house have two baths?

7. CONSONANTS / lz, mz, nz, ŋz, rz /

Words Frequently Used

Below are some nouns ending in /lz/, /mz/, /nz/, /ŋz/, and /rz/ in their possessive and plural forms, made by adding the "z sound" to the singular form of the nouns. Practice these words containing final consonant clusters.

names	nouns	things	pencils
Jim's	Jane's	rings	cars
times	pens	walls	ears
poems	songs	smiles	letters
towns	king's	schools	chairs

Sentences

6. How many times have you played these games?
7. These signs say there are telephones in this drugstore.
8. What are the king's favorite songs?
9. The walls of these schools are made of brick.
10. Do you get many letters from your sisters and brothers?

8. CONSONANTS / bz, dz, gz, vz, ðz /

Words Frequently Used

Below are some verbs ending in /bz/, /dz/, /gz/, /vz/, and /ðz/ in the third person singular, present tense form. Practice these words containing final consonant clusters.

robs	leads	digs	believes	breathes
rubs	reads	brags	lives	bathes
describes	decides	begs	leaves	smooths
grabs	rides	hugs	arrives	

Sentences

11. This book describes Washington, D.C.
12. He sometimes reads while he rides on the bus.

13. Every day John begs us to go with him.
14. The teacher always gives him a book when he arrives.
15. He usually bathes at nine o'clock.

9. FINAL CONSONANT CLUSTERS

Review Sentences

Review the sentences you have practiced in PD 35.

A. Sentences with / bz /, / dz /, / gz /, / vz /, and / ðz / in nouns
   1. Bob's sister has two jobs.
   2. These beds are more comfortable than Ed's.
   3. Both the dog's legs are hurt.
   4. Mr. Ives and Mr. Cleaves have been friends all their lives.
   5. Does the new house have two baths?

B. Sentences with / lz /, / mz /, / nz /, / ŋz / and / rz / in nouns
   6. How many times have you played these games?
   7. These signs say there are telephones in this drugstore.
   8. What are the king's favorite songs?
   9. The walls of these schools are made of brick.
   10. Do you get many letters from your sisters and brothers?

C. Sentences with / bz /, / dz /, / gz /, / vz /, and / ðz /
   11. This book describes Washington, D.C.
   12. He sometimes reads while he rides on the bus.
   13. Every day John begs us to go with him.
   14. The teacher always gives him a book when he arrives.
   15. He usually bathes at nine o'clock.

PRONUNCIATION DRILL 36

10. CONSONANTS / mz, nz, ŋz, lz, rz /

Words Frequently Used

Below are some verbs ending in /mz/, /nz/, /ŋz/, /lz/, and /rz/ in the third person singular, present tense form. Practice these words containing final consonant clusters.

comes	runs	sings	falls	wears
seems	begins	rings	feels	hears
dreams	cleans	brings	pulls	appears
screams	turns	bangs	smiles	interferes

Sentences

1. It seems that he always comes to class late.
2. The class begins at nine o'clock.
3. The postman always rings the doorbell when he brings us letters.
4. Ask him how he feels today.
5. She always hears the news on the radio.

11. CONSONANTS / bd, jd, gd, vd, ðd /

Words Frequently Used

Below are some verbs ending in /bd/, /jd/, /gd/, /vd/, and /ðd/ in the past tense form. Practice these words containing final consonant clusters.

robbed	engaged	lagged	believed	breathed
rubbed	judged	bragged	lived	bathed
grabbed	urged	begged	received	smoothed
described	obliged	hugged	arrived	

Sentences

6. This criminal robbed a bank.
7. Dr. Black charged $5.00 for that treatment.
8. We begged them to stay with us.
9. He received the letter when he arrived.
10. She stood beside the window and breathed the fresh air.

12. CONSONANTS / md, nd, ŋd /

Words Frequently Used

Below are some verbs ending in /md/, /nd/, and /ŋd/ in the past tense form. Practice these words ending in consonant clusters.

seemed	learned	longed (for)
dreamed	cleaned	belonged
named	turned	clanged
warmed	rained	banged

Sentences

11. They seemed to enjoy the movie very much.
12. He learned English when he returned to the United States.
13. The little boy banged the door.

13. CONSONANTS / zd, ld, rd /

Words Frequently Used

Below are some verbs ending in /zd/, /ld/, and /rd/ in their past tense form. Practice these words containing final consonant clusters.

advised	called	heard
closed	pulled	appeared
amazed	killed	cleared
surprised	smiled	lowered

Sentences

14. I closed the door because I supposed you had gone.
15. Robert called for Louise at eight o'clock.
16. I heard every word you said.

14. FINAL CONSONANT CLUSTERS

Review Sentences

Review the sentences you have practiced in PD 36.

A. Sentences with / mz /, / nz /, / ŋz /, / lz /, and / rz /

1. It seems that he always comes to class late.
2. The class begins at nine o'clock.
3. The postman always rings the doorbell when he brings us letters.
4. Ask him how he feels today.
5. She always hears the news on the radio.

B. Sentences with / bd /, / jd /, / gd /, / vd /, and / ðd /

6. This criminal robbed a bank.
7. Dr. Black charged $5.00 for that treatment.
8. We begged them to stay with us.
9. He received the letter when he arrived.
10. She stood beside the window and breathed the fresh air.

C. Sentences with / md /, / nd /, and / ŋd /

11. They seemed to enjoy the movie very much.
12. He learned English when he returned to the United States.
13. The little boy banged the door.

D. Sentences with / zd /, / ld /, and / rd /

14. I closed the door because I supposed you had gone.
15. Robert called for Louise at eight o'clock.
16. I heard every word you said.

GROUP XVI | **Letters and Sounds**

PRONUNCIATION DRILL 37

THE ALPHABET

Review the forms of the *capital letters, small letters,* and *names of the letters* of the English alphabet.

Capital Letter	*Small Letter*	*Name of Letter*
A	a	/ey/
B	b	/biy/
C	c	/siy/
D	d	/diy/
E	e	/iy/
F	f	/ef/
G	g	/jiy/
H	h	/eyč/
I	i	/ay/
J	j	/jey/
K	k	/key/
L	l	/el/
M	m	/em/
N	n	/en/
O	o	/ow/

P	p	/piy/
Q	q	/kyuw/
R	r	/ar/
S	s	/es/
T	t	/tiy/
U	u	/yuw/
V	v	/viy/
W	w	/dəbɨlyùw/
X	x	/eks/
Y	y	/way/
Z	z	/ziy/ (British /zed/)

1. Repeat the capital letters.
2. Repeat the small letters.
3. Then say the alphabet backwards.
4. Listen to the alphabet song which American children sing.

ABCDEFG
HIJKLMNOP
Q and R and S and T
UVWXYZ
Now you've heard my ABC's
Won't you say them for me please.

USES OF THE NAMES OF THE LETTERS

There are various occasions when it is necessary to use the names of the letters and their plurals. The plural of a letter of the alphabet is usually written 's (apostrophe "s" /əpástrəfiy és/). The plural s is pronounced /s, z, ɨz/, according to the last sound of the singular. Say the following plurals:

/s/	f - f's
/ɨz/	h - h's, s - s's, x - x's
/z/	a - a's, b's, c's, d's, e's, g's, i's, j's, k's, l's, m's, n's, o's, p's, q's, r's t's, u's, v's, w's, y's, z's

143

Sentences

1. My teacher gave me three A's and two B's for my work in class.
2. *MISSISSIPPI* is spelled with four *s's* and two *p's*.
3. His name is John Doe — capital *j-o-h-n,* capital *d-o-e.*
4. The vowel letters are *a, e, i, o, u,* and sometimes *y* and *w.*
5. The following are the consonant letters: *b c d, f g h, j k l m n, p q r s t, v w x y z.*

USE OF THE ALPHABET IN ABBREVIATIONS

There are three common types of abbreviations in English:

1. The *Mr.* type of abbreviation (pronunciation of abbreviation - pronunciation of complete form)

Abbreviation	Pronunciation	Full Form
Mr.	/místər/	Mister
Dr.	/dáktər/	Doctor
Maj.	/méyjər/	Major
Jr.	/júwnyər/	Junior
Dept.	/dipártmɨnt/	Department
Ave.	/ǽvɨn(y)uw/	Avenue
Mrs.	/mísɨz/	(Mistress)
Ms.	/miz/	(see Note below)
st.	/striyt/	street
St.	/seynt/	saint
lb., lbs.	/páwnd/, /páwndz/	pound pounds
oz.	/áwnts/, /áwntsɨz/	ounce, ounces

NOTE: Although *Mrs.,* pronounced /misɨz/, is the abbreviation for *mistress,* mistress is never used as a title now. *Ms.* /miz/ is now commonly used as a general title for all women. It does not imply any particular marital status, as do Miss and Mrs. The abbreviations *lb.* and *oz.* are really abbreviations of non-English words.

2. The *UNESCO* type of abbreviation (abbreviation is pronounced like a word)

Abbreviation	Pronunciation	Full Form
UNESCO	/yunéskow/	*U*nited *N*ations *E*ducational, *S*cientific, and *C*ultural *O*rganization
WAC	/wæk/	The *W*omen's *A*rmy *C*orps
CARE	/kehr/	The *C*o-operative for *A*merican *R*emittances to *E*urope
OPEC	/ówpek/	*O*rganization of *P*etroleum *E*xporting *C*ountries

3. The *M.D.* type of abbreviation (pronunciation of abbreviation - names of letters in abbreviation)

Abbreviation	Pronunciation	Full Form
M.D.	/èm díy/	Medicinae Doctor
B.A.	/bìy éy/	Bachelor of Arts
B.S.	/bìy és/	Bachelor of Science
M.A.	/èm éy/	Master of Arts
Ph.D.	/pìy èyc díy/	Philosophiae Doctor
YMCA	/wày em sìy éy/	Young Men's Christian Association
UFO	/yùw èf ów/	Unidentified Flying Object
TVA	/tìy vìy éy/	Tennessee Valley Authority
TWA	/tìy dəbɨlyuw éy/	Trans-World Airlines
ABC	/èy bìy síy/	American Broadcasting Company
CBS	/sìy bìy és/	Columbia Broadcasting System
NBC	/èn bìy síy/	National Broadcasting Company
AFL	/èy èf él/	American Federation of Labor
C.I.O.	/sìy ày ów/	Congress of Industrial Organizations
N.A.M.	/èn èy ém/	National Association of Manufacturers

THE ENGLISH ALPHABET AND
ENGLISH PRONUNCIATION

The twenty-six letters of the English alphabet are used to represent the twenty-four consonant sounds and a minimum of fourteen vowel sounds. The following are some important things to know about how English spelling corresponds to English pronunciation.

1. The short vowel sounds are regularly represented by VC(C).[1]

    back   pet   tip   knot   us

To represent the short vowel sound when you add a suffix beginning with a vowel (for example, *-ing, -er, -est*), double the final consonant letter if the word ends in one consonant.

    pat, patting   pet, petting   tip, tipping   knot, knotted

No spelling changes are made if the word ends in two consonants.

    back, backer   bend, bending   tick, ticking
    knock, knocking   rust, rusty

2. The long vowels are regularly represented by VC*e*.

    bake   Pete   type   note   use

Such words regularly lose the final *e* before a suffix beginning with a vowel.

    bake, baking   type, typist   note, noted   use, using

NOTE: The long vowels are also represented by other spellings. See PD 38.

3. Words which end in C*y* change the *y* to *i* before the ending *-es*.

    baby, babies   city, cities   family, families
    try, tries   fly, flies

---

[1]V=*vowel*; C=*consonant*

4. English spelling often uses two or more letters to represent one sound or no sound. (The letters in parentheses represent a single sound.)

(CH, TCH):	cheap, each, match
(CK):	pick, lack, lock
(DG-E):	bridge, judging
(GH):	cough, enough, through, bough, ought, thorough
(GN):	gnat, gnaw, sign
(KN):	knife, knock
(MB):	comb, lamb
(NG):	sing, singer
(PH):	phone, philosophy, graph
(SH):	ship, fish
(SI, SU):	measure, vision
(SSI, TI):	mission, nation
(TH) /ð/:	then, mother, bathe, smooth
(TH) /θ/:	thin, mathematical, truth
(WR):	wrong, awry, write

THE ALPHABET AND THE VOWEL SOUNDS OF ENGLISH

You have studied the twenty vowel sounds represented by the five vowel letters, alone and in combination, as in the words below.

1		2		3		4	
/i/	pit	/iy/	Pete			/ih/	peer
/e/	pet	/ey/	pate			/eh/	pare
/æ/	pat						
/ə/	putt					/əh/	purr
/a/	pot	/ay/	pie	/aw/	bout	/ah/	par
/ɔ/	dog						
/u/	put			/uw/	boot	/uh/	poor
/o/	port	/oy/	boy	/ow/	boat	/oh/	pour

All these vowel sounds are in loud stressed syllables.

In quiet unstressed syllables, the two most common vowel sounds are "the short *u* sound" /ə/, as in *butter*; and "the barred-*i* sound" /ɨ/, as in *children, little, roses,* and *just a minute.*

The "barred-*i* sound" (represented by the letter *i* and a bar superimposed) is extremely frequent:

children	/čildrɨn/ or /čɨldrɨn/
roses	/rowzɨz/
just a minute	/jɨst ə minɨt/

THE ALPHABET AND THE CONSONANT SOUNDS OF ENGLISH

The twenty-one consonant letters of the English alphabet are used alone and in the combinations you studied in the two previous sections to represent the twenty-four consonant sounds. These sounds are represented by different symbols in different books (θ, th; đ, ŧħ, dh, ð; sh, zh, ž; ch, č; f; j, g, dz; ng, ŋ, etc.). The symbols are not important, if you can say and understand the sounds perfectly.

In each key word below, the letters which represent one of the twenty-four English consonant sounds are underlined.

The Consonant Sounds of English

/p/	a**pp**le	/t/	li**tt**le	/c/	kit**ch**en	/k/	pi**ck**le
/b/	ru**bb**er	/d/	bo**d**y	/j/	a**j**ar	/g/	bi**gg**er
/f/	tele**ph**one	/θ/	e**th**er	/s/	cla**ss**ify	/š/	na**ti**on
/v/	e**v**er	/ð/	mo**th**er	/z/	ea**s**y	/ž/	vi**si**on
/m/	gra**mm**ar	/n/	ba**n**ana	/y/	Mala**y**a	/ŋ/	si**ng**er
/w/	a**w**ay	/l/,/r/	ear**l**y			/h/	re**h**earse

PRONUNCIATION DRILL 38

English spelling is irregular, especially the spelling of the vowel sounds. All spelling rules have exceptions, and these exceptions often occur in words which are frequently used. In the following lessons you will study the spelling of the short and long vowel sounds, of the vowel sounds before *r*, and of the consonants.

148

1. THE SHORT AND LONG i SOUNDS

The spelling of the "short *i* sound" /i/, as in *pit,* and the "long *i* sound" /ay/, as in *bite.*

The "short *i* sound" /i/ is regularly spelled *i*C.

bit   quit   fin   sit   did   tip

It is sometimes spelled *y*.

rhythm   mystery   myth

The "long *i* sound" /ay/ is regularly spelled *i*Ce, *y, y*Ce, *ie,* or *igh*.

*i*Ce:	bite, quite, fine
y:	by, cry
*y*Ce:	type
ie:	die, lie
igh:	high, night

This sound is often spelled *y* when it is final in words of one syllable.

by   cry   try   dry

Notice the difference in spelling and pronunciation in the pairs of words below:

Short i	Long i
bit	bite
sit	site or sight
quit	quite
fin	fine
did	died
tip	type

2. THE SHORT AND LONG e SOUNDS

The spelling of the "short *e* sound" /e/, as in *pet*, and the "long *e* sound" /iy/, as in *Pete.*

The "short e sound" is regularly spelled eC.

    met   led   fed   ferry

The "short e sound" is often spelled ea.

bread	head	heavy
dead	weather	measure
dread	heaven	wealth

Common exceptions are *says, said*.

The "long e sound" /iy/ is regularly spelled eCe, ee, or ea.

    Pete, concrete   meet, feet   meat, breathe

The letter *y* has the "long e sound" at the end of polysyllabic words like the following:

    happily   merry   healthy   easy   lovely

Notice the difference in spelling and pronunciation in the pairs of words below:

Short e	*Long e*
met	meet or meat
fed	feed
set	seat
bet	beet or beat
bread	breed
dead	deed
pet	Pete

3. THE SHORT AND LONG a SOUNDS

The spelling of the "short a sound" /æ/, as in *pat*, and the "long a sound" /ey/, as in *tape*.

The "short a sound" /æ/ is regularly spelled aC.

```
tap     pass    can
lack    sad     pal
bath    Sam     cap
```

The "long *a* sound" /ey/, is regularly spelled *aCe, ay, ai, ey,* or *ei.*

aCe: tape, lake, bathe, same, cane, pale
ay: pay, say, play, day
ai: sail, mail, pail
ey: they, convey
ei: veil, eight, neighbor, vein

Notice the difference in spelling and pronunciation in the pairs of words below:

Short a	Long a
tap	tape
cap	cape
lack	lake
pass	pace
bath	bathe
pal	pale
at	ate or eight
van	vain, vein, or vane

4. THE SHORT AND LONG o SOUNDS

The spelling of the "short *o* sounds" /a/, as in *pot*, or /ɔ/, as in *dog*, and the "long *o* sound" /ow/, as in *know*.

The "short *o* sounds" /a/ or /ɔ/ are regularly spelled *oC*.

```
not     smock   long
rob     fox     cloth
cop     cost    office
                often
```

The "long *o* sound" is regularly spelled *oCe, oa, ow,* and *ou.*

oCe:	note, robe, cope, smoke
oa:	boat, coat, throat, soap
ow:	bowl, sow, grow, know
ou:	soul, shoulder

Notice the differences in spelling and pronunciation in the pairs of words below:

Short o	Long o
not	note
rob	robe
cop	cope
smock	smoke
fox	folks
cost	coast
cloth	clothe

5. THE SHORT AND LONG u SOUNDS AND THE SHORT oo SOUND

The spelling of the "short u sound" /ə/, as in *but*; the "long u sounds" /uw/ or /yuw/, as in *who* and *cute*; and the "short oo sound" /u/, as in *put*.

There is not really a regular spelling for the "short u sound." It is usually spelled uC, *ou,* or *o.*

uC:	cut, us, tub, run, rush, rub, mud, much, luck
ou:	country, double, enough, trouble, rough, tough
o:	come, some, govern, nothing, other, brother, mother, love, glove, done, does, month, son, front, money

There are also several spellings for the "long u sounds." They are spelled uCe (or another vowel), *ew, ui,* or *o.*

uCe:	June, July, use, usually, music, human
ew:	news, knew, few
ui:	fruit, juice, suit
o:	who, move, prove

152

Other spellings are used in *Tuesday, beauty, beautiful.*

The /u/ sound, as in *took*, is spelled with *oo*C or *u*C.

*oo*C: took, cook, book, shook, look, good, stood, hood, wood, foot

*u*C: put, pull, bull, full, bush, push, cushion, butcher

6. SPELLING OF VOWEL SOUNDS FOLLOWED BY r

Spelling of /ihr/, as in *here*; /ehr/, as in *air*; /ohr/ or /ɔhr/, as in *four*; /uhr/, as in *tour*; /ahr/, as in *part*; and /əhr/ as in *girl*.

/ihr/ is spelled *ear, eer,* or *ere.*

ear: ear, clear, dear, fear
eer: cheer, beer, queer, career
ere: merely, here, adhere, interfere

/ehr/ is spelled *air, are, ear, ere,* or *eir.*

air: air, pair, chair, fair, stairs
are: fare, care, share, rare
ear: wear, bear, pear, tear
ere: there, where
eir: their, heir

/ohr/ and /ɔhr/ are spelled *or, oor, our,* or *ar*:

or: or, for
oor: floor, door
our: four, pour
ar: war, warm

/uhr/ is spelled *ure, oor, our. ure* is usually pronounced /yuhr/.

ure: sure, cure, pure
oor: poor, boor
our: your, tour

/ahr/ is regularly spelled *ar*(C); sometimes *ear*.

ar(C):	are, March, large, car, park, farm
ear:	heart

/əhr/ is spelled *ur, ir, er, (w)or,* or *ear*C.

ur:	burn, turn, hurry, hurt
ir:	thirteen, thirty, girl, sir, first
er:	her, were, person, verb
(w)or:	work, word, worry, world, worth
*ear*C:	heard, earth, learn, earn

PRONUNCIATION DRILL 39

1. SPELLING OF CONSONANT SOUNDS

The spelling of the consonant sounds in which one sound is regularly
represented by one letter.

/b/	B	boy, big; able, horrible; job
/d/	D	date, dime; ready, older; bad, good
/g/	G	game, go; bigger, cigarette; rug, dig
/h/	H	hat, health; behind, anyhow
/l/	L	live, leave; finally, lately; will, fill
/m/	M	might, may; important, grammar; home, same
/p/	P	pay, picture; happy, apply; up, cap
/t/	T	time, terrible; little, butter; ate, at
/v/	V	very, vegetable; every, flavor; give, have
/w/	W	will, world; away, anyway

2. SPELLING OF CONSONANT SOUNDS

Spelling of the consonant sounds which are regularly represented by one
of several letters, or a combination of letters.

/f/	F or	find, found; awful, careful; if, off;
	PH	philosophy; telephone; graph
/n/	N or	nice, near; many, money; man, men;
	KN or	knife, know, knowledge;
	GN	gnat, gnu
/r/	R or	read, room; Mary, wearing; car, are;
	WR	write, wrote
/k/	C	The letter *c* regularly represents /k/ before *a, o,* and *u,* and before *l* and r.
		cat, cop, cute; class, clear; cream, critical
	K	The letter *k* has only one sound, /k/, and is regularly used before *e* and *i;* after *l, n,* and *r;* with "long" vowels; and *oo.*
	CK	*ck* represents the /k/ in the middle or at the end of words.
		Ken, kettle; kiss, kill; milk, silk; dark, work; thank, ink; cheek, leak, soak, break, cake, like, coke, Luke, look, took; black, deck, block, tick
/s/	S or	The letter *s* represents two sounds, /s/ and /z/ (see below).
	C	The letter *c* also represents two sounds, /k/ (see above) and /s/.
		The letter *c* regularly represents the /s/ sound when it is used before *e* and *i.*
		say, see; sister, missing; bus, yes; cell, circle; recess, placing; peace, ice
/z/	Z or S	The letter *z* has only one sound, /z/. The letter *s* has two sounds, /s/ at the beginning of words, and /s/ or /z/ in the middle or at the end of words: zoo, zero; fuzzy, lazy; size, prize; easy, busy; lose, these
/j/	J or G	The letter *j* has only one sound and is used at the beginning of words. *g* has two, /j/ and /g/.
		g regularly represents /j/ before *e* and *i* (common exceptions: get, give, girl, and their derivatives).
		jelly, jam; George, genius; raging, ginger; cage, large

/š/	SH	The letters *sh* regularly represent the /š/ sound, but in the middle of words, the letters *ti* often represent this sound: shoe, share; wishing, cushion; dish, fish, nation, condition, action, fiction
/č/	CH	The letters *ch* regularly represent the /č/ sound, but in the middle of words, the letter *t* often occurs instead: church, child; kitchen, itching; each, such; nature, culture, actual, ritual
/θ/	TH	think, thanks; nothing, something; breath, birth
/ð/	TH	this, that; mother, father; bathe, clothe
/y/	Y or U	you, your; beyond, unyielding (See Section 5 of this PD for *u* spelling.)
/ŋ/	NG	This sound never occurs at the beginning of English words: singer, ringing; thing, long
/ž/	S or G	This sound never occurs at the beginning of English words. In the middle of words, it is usually represented by *s*V, and at the end of words by *g*V. measure, vision; rouge, garage

Note the following combinations of consonant sounds: /kw/ is regularly represented by the letters *qu*; quick, quiet, quite. In the middle and at the end of words, /ks/ is sometimes represented by the letter *x*: Mexico, excellent; tax, box.